MANAGING THE
QUARTER
LIFE [CRISIS]

Weetjie

Die boek het vir my nogal nice
gelyk vir ons probleem om besluite te
neem agv die oneindig baie opsies wat
daar is om van te kies.
Ek gaan ook die boek lees en hopelik
voel 'n mens 'n bietjie beter oor jouself.
Lekker lees!
Baie liefde Hettie

To Richard
As it began, so it continues…

First published in 2003 by
Struik Publishers
(a division of New Holland Publishing (South Africa) (Pty) Ltd)
Cornelis Struik House
80 McKenzie Street
Cape Town 8001

New Holland Publishing is a member of the Johnnic Publishing Group

10 9 8 7 6 5 4 3 2 1

Publishing Manager: Linda de Villiers
Editor: Ethné Clark
Designer: Sean Robertson
Illustrator: David du Plessis

www.struik.co.za

Reproduction by Hirt & Carter (Pty) Ltd
Printed and bound by Pinetown Printers (Pty) Ltd

ISBN 1 86872 845 5

Log on to our photographic website
www.imagesofafrica.co.za for an African experience

[contents]

[introduction]

As with everything else in my life up to this point, I was determined that my wedding would be a carefully organised bit of choreography. I had been planning the event for months, and even the tiniest detail was carefully orchestrated, right down to the part where I would sing the first few verses of the song for the first dance. About two minutes into the song, my new husband, Richard, would stroll onto the dance floor, sweep me up in his arms, and twirl me around in our show-stopping, carefully rehearsed, dance number.

I know this seems like the ideal setting for something to go horribly wrong. You're waiting to hear that I tripped on my dress, or forgot the lyrics, or felt an unbridled urge to sneeze during the chorus. But nothing did go wrong. In fact, it was the most perfect night of my life and it went off without a single visible hitch. It was the night when every romantic bone in my body got its just deserts, when every harp-bearing cherub applauded at the angelic beauty of it all. But... it was also the night that I reinforced the most astounding realisation of my adult life so far: I was 27, about to start a life with a wonderful man, all the stars apparently in alignment... and

I had absolutely no idea where my life was going. On that night, during one of those perfect moments, I realised that I had no inkling of what tomorrow would hold. I didn't even know where we would be spending our first night as a married couple and, thanks to recent adventures and changes in our lives, I had no idea where my new husband and I were even going to settle. So my wedding night was also the night I met my very own Quarterlife Crisis face to face. From then on, we were constant companions.

I had woken up early on the morning of my wedding to practise my lines. By the end of that enchanted night, I had realised that there was no script for what was coming next: my home, my work, my identity, my dreams – they were all about to be transformed, yet I wasn't sure how. I was about to be thrust into the throes of that crisis that hits 20–35ers when they least expect it. It's the crisis that is born, at least partly, of multiple possibilities: too many career options, too many different places to live, too many potential identities. It's a crisis that bites as we leave a flippant young-adulthood behind and venture into the wilds of being a 'proper' grown-up. It's a crisis that makes us consider big issues when we'd really rather not. It's a modern crisis, inspired by the technological boom which has turned some of our peers into renowned success stories by an age at which they might even be turned away at some nightclubs for being too young. It's a crisis which too few realise they are going through, leaving them feeling alone, inept and frustrated. Certainly, these are the feelings I was left to contend with as the magic of my wedding night, and my life leading up to it, began to make way for my amorphous future.

The more I think and talk about the concept of the Quarterlife Crisis, the more I realise how common it is. In fact, I have very few friends between the ages of 20 and 35 who aren't contending with the very same questions I seem to face every day in this phase of my life:

What career should I focus on? It seems that there are numerous possibilities, and I have multiple interests. Or maybe I should travel now and explore the world before I become too entrenched in a career. But if I do that, will I be left behind my peers in the race for success?

Where should I live? And for how long? Should I stay with my family, follow my friends, or blaze my own trail?

Shouldn't I be more 'settled' by this stage in my life? Is it OK to still be experimenting with my life's options?

I'm too old for 'spin-the-bottle' but too young for a Midlife Crisis. **Where do I belong?**

Am I useless just because I can't define what my life's dream is?

Don't people **expect** bigger and better things from me at this stage?

What if I **try something new and I fail?**

Why is it that **everyone seems surer of themselves than me?**

For the most part, it seems that Quarterlifers stew in silent agony, waiting for the answers to dawn on them or striving to push through a growing sense of discomfort at the current state of their lives. They are often unaware that they are going through such a 'crisis' and they very seldom talk about it to others. In their silence, they miss out on the heartening realisation that they are not alone, that others are enduring similar situations in which their life's ambition, meaning and status quo are being called into question, and that living through the crisis is most of the battle won.

I've been bulldozing my way down this Quarterlife path for a while now, and along the route, have come to some understanding of what it takes to make your way through it. In the spirit of collaboration which I've found so useful in tackling my own Quarterlife Crisis, I would like to share my story with you; so you'll find it – or at least parts of it – in the next few chapters. This book then goes on to discuss the various elements of the Quarterlife Crisis, taking an in-depth look at the conditions of modern life that have helped generate such a condition. And because I know that what you are probably looking for are answers, I have put forward some suggestions for managing this phase of life and making it work. Truth be told, though, there are no hard and fast rules, so what I hope to do is extend solidarity through my own story and share some of the insights and solutions that I've found to be useful. I hope you will too.

You will find that my story talks a lot about achievements. I've always been a hard worker, and achieving – or overachieving – has become a way of life. But in a way, that's part of what made Quarterlife such a difficult time for me – because the Quarterlife Crisis came as such a shock. It truly is the great leveller: overachievers and underachievers, hard workers and slackers, academics and party animals may all find themselves at the gates of this indiscriminate crisis. My experience and analysis of it has brought me to this point: sharing insights, proposing ideas, and hoping that others will take heart when they face their own reality.

So this book is for every Quarterlifer out there, for everyone who might have encountered a Quarterlifer and found them unfathomable, and for every person who aims to meet, endure and relish that wonderful, horrible, inevitable phase we call Quarterlife.

A CRISIS [is born]

I have always had ambitions. The ones that I had when I was really young were perhaps the most vibrant and powerful of them all. While other kids were moaning about homework and dancing with hairbrushes instead of microphones in front of the mirror, I was probably correcting my English essay and dreaming about how I'd change things if I ever became a prefect at my school. In fact, every dream I'd ever had paled in comparison to the moment I was announced head prefect of my high school. Every childish aspiration I'd ever entertained shimmered, fizzled and was extinguished as I walked, dumbfounded, across the school stage that day towards my grinning headmaster to accept the leadership badge. The blue blazer that I earned as head prefect was my pinnacle, my Olympic torch, my goal weight. And that day is one I will never forget.

Since then, I've always compared my life's accomplishments to that grand one of my adolescence. Becoming head prefect was the stuff of my fantasies – at least since age 12 when I had stopped dreaming about a Barbie playhouse or meeting the members of Wham! Nothing else came close to approximating my excitement and sense of accomplishment: not even being given the lead role in the school play, nor winning national competitions, nor acing my final exams. The day I became head prefect of 2,500 students became the benchmark against which I measured everything else to come.

Life according to plan

That was how life was back then. I went to school, understood what I needed to do in order to move through the ranks, and progressed from year to year. Sometimes things took me by surprise, but never to the point that they threw me off my well-chartered map. Life had always gone according to plan and, since it was logical that I would move on to university in this same organised, well-planned manner, I didn't worry about the future too much and focused on enjoying my school days.

I left high school with a bang and entered the hallowed halls of university life. My first day there was much like my first day of school. Nervous and feeling like a little kid, I stared worriedly at the ivy-covered buildings and the returning students, wondering if I would ever again feel that sense of belonging and accomplishment that I had enjoyed at school – suddenly, being head prefect meant very little. But it didn't take me long to settle in, particularly since I lived in a university residence and felt an immediate bond with the other first-year students. Nor did it take me long to seek out a lucky packet of activities, and by the end of my first month I had stacked up a host of committees, societies and social groups to join, and soon I was back in positions of leadership and accomplishment.

Although high school remained the apex, university was certainly measuring up to my hopes and expectations. I had some vague ideas of what I might want to become one day: I toyed with law, but found it too inhumane to really have people's interests at heart; I dabbled with foreign languages which I had always enjoyed, but couldn't see a future for myself there; I fell in love with psychology and maintained the subject as a focus during my years at university. Above all, I revelled in the luxury of study for study's sake. I studied whatever interested me (what else could explain the half course in Greek mythology?) and thrived. I did have to give up some long-harboured dreams: like when I joined the university choir and quickly learned that my few minutes of yodelling in the shower was no match for the aspiring pro's that had also joined up. So bang went my sideline singing career. But I digress…

Undergraduate studies came to an end and my passion for English and psychology begged for further exploration. I chose to take my interest in the study of human nature to the next level and went on to do an honours degree in psychology. I didn't think about it too much. It seemed obvious that, since I was enjoying the subject so much, I should take it one step further. Eventually, I graduated from university with an undergraduate degree Cum Laude, a post-graduate degree Cum Laude, and a bunch of titles, medals and leadership positions to stuff the pockets of that old blue blazer. I had to admit that I had generally come to define myself as an achiever, and would be disappointed if I neglected my goals. But I never expected achievement, I just hoped for it.

The impostor complex

So there I was, nearing the end of an extremely gratifying postgraduate degree, with the whole wide world open in front of me. I felt sad to be leaving university, in the same way that I had been sad to leave school. Aside from the attachments with the people and the place, I knew that leaving meant putting aside everything I had accomplished again, creeping out of a comfort zone that had quickly become warm and fuzzy, and starting all over. I've never been good at saying goodbye and these crossover points in my life really felt like mammoth farewells. Although I had mostly done well at my endeavours, I never counted on it and felt a fluttering of fear that I might not achieve in the future as I had in the past. 'Maybe this time, everyone will find out that I'm not as clever or capable as they think I am…' In psychology, this is referred to as the 'impostor complex' – the feeling that you may just be a fraud, that you are not actually as accomplished and as able as you appear, and that you should fear being exposed.

I knew that I had some excellent grounding in psychology, but I didn't feel certain about it as a final choice of career (and the interviewers for the clinical psychology master's degree are notoriously scary, with an uncanny ability to pick up even the smallest lack of certainty or absolute dedication to the degree and profession). I knew that the master's degree was probably a logical next step, but all my lecturers and mentors seemed to feel that some life experience would be an invaluable asset to acquire before even applying for the course. But before I could become too overwhelmed by all of this, and even before I had really given myself time to think about 'what next', I was presented with an interesting option.

Entering the real world

I received a letter from a management consulting company which invited me (and scores of other cold-called recipients, of course) to consider management consulting as a career path. It promised exposure to multiple industries, the chance to acquire business skills without the prerequisite of a business degree, access to superior training and development programmes, and so on. It all seemed rather glamorous and, having grown up in a family obsessed with business (but never having felt particularly drawn to it before), this seemed like an ideal opportunity to acquire new skills and experience, with minimal risk. After all, I was still young – there was no need to be making final life decisions just yet and a few years in consulting might really show me the way towards where I ultimately wanted to be.

And just like that, the next step fell into place for me. I was interviewed by a few companies, cringed at the rejection phone calls, screeched at the acceptance phone calls, and made my way into the innards of a huge management consulting firm.

The old 'first day at school' feeling was no stranger to me at the start of my job. This was an entirely unfamiliar environment and I had to get used to the new rules and norms.

During my first week of work, I remember asking the Human Resources Manager if I could leave half an hour early one day to take my family to the airport, solemnly negotiating to work in the extra half-hour over lunch. She (unsuccessfully) held back a bemused smile and agreed, then couldn't contain her amusement any longer and said, 'School is out, honey. No need to ask for permission anymore – although I do enjoy giving a good caning once in a while!'

I was far away from my head prefect days, but the survival and over achiever instincts kicked in soon enough. So at the end of my first year at the firm, I already belonged to two in-house committees and was a keen participant in the optional extras that came along. I got promoted within the minimum time frame and received lots of positive feedback from my managers. I thoroughly enjoyed my project work, interaction with my colleagues and clients, and the challenge of a high-paced, exciting new realm. Of course there were numerous knocks to my blue blazer confidence, but nothing from which I felt I couldn't bounce back and learn. I struggled a bit with the lifestyle requirements: lots of travel (which seemed glamorous at first but the lure of collecting air miles fade with the smell of too many hired cars), constant uncertainty regarding the next project (which was difficult for someone like me who claims to be the rightful inventor of the old boy scout motto – 'be prepared'), and long hours (which was both an element of the organisation's culture and a personal demand). Other than that, though, the career path was well defined – the hierarchy of positions in the firm was clear and you knew exactly what was required in order to move up the corporate ladder. I liked that sense of knowing. I appreciated that my expectations were actively managed and felt that clearly defined goals would become achievable ones (hmmm – I really do sound like a consultant here!). Certainly, the self-growth was intense and I was very content with my lot in life.

A new perspective

Two years on, while I was happily floating along in my mostly satisfying consultant existence, my boyfriend, Richard, lit a slow-growing fire under my fast-growing bum. At the time, a whole bunch of our friends was going over to the UK. To 'do the London thing' has almost become tradition among my peers, many of whom spend at least a year (generally after studying) earning sterling, experiencing what it's like to live in a foreign country and travelling. In fact, London is brimming with, in particular, South Africans, Australians and New Zealanders doing this very thing. Richard wondered out loud why we weren't doing the same.

'Imagine what it would be like to live somewhere completely new, under our own steam, with Europe around the corner for quick weekend breaks,' he said.

Richard and I had been dating for about four years and I had come to know his adventurous streak that yearns for the extreme and seeks the occasional adrenalin rush. Usually, he satisfies it by surfing unsurfable waves, climbing unclimbable mountains or growing his hair to an annoy-my-mother length. I laughed. Us, rip up our lives to go and spend time in a cold, rainy city where the streets all have the same names?

'That's ridiculous, Richard, I'm perfectly happy in my job and you've only been in yours for a year.'

But I somehow knew that this wasn't a fleeting fantasy of his, and over the next few days he wove an attractive proposal, conjuring up romantic images of Paris on the weekend, the Colosseum at sunset, and tulips in Amsterdam. You must know by now that I am not someone who likes change; I have no problem parking securely in a comfort zone. I probably would have stayed in my consulting job forever and a day if Richard hadn't jolted me into a fantasy world of travel, foreign living and Harrods on demand.

I grappled with the concept for weeks: would it be sensible to give up this really good job for a year or two of what might or might not be valuable experience? How would I afford to live in London if I couldn't find a good job straight away? Is travel necessarily a good experience in itself? People say that by travelling you learn so much about yourself and the way of the world. But would that actually make a difference to my life? At age 25, shouldn't I be focusing on my career rather than gallivanting around the world? Or maybe this would be the time to play rookie for a bit and not take things so seriously – there'd be time enough for the serious stuff.

Backwards and forwards I went. My parents would be wholly encouraging of whatever I chose to do (which in a way made the decision more difficult; sometimes it's hard not having someone tell you what to do). My friends were really keen on the idea and some others even decided to take the plunge and go to London too. But I struggled with what to do about my job. I had been enjoying my role even though I wasn't entirely convinced that this was what I wanted to do for the rest of my life. I felt nervous to set the change ball rolling and wrestled with familiar questions of self-belief. Would I be able to find work in London? What if I wasn't any good at what I was doing? What if I was miserable overseas and the move ruined my relationship? Wouldn't my blue blazer just get moth-eaten if I left it, and this life, behind? So I took myself off to my mentor in the firm and put the idea to him. To some people, like my mentor, the choice was a no-brainer. 'You're young, with no commitments to keep you at home, you should definitely take the opportunity. And the chance to get this working visa won't be available for long.' He came up with a suggestion that seemed to make the whole dilemma go away: I could take a 'leave of absence' from my job at the company (essentially an extended vacation), go off to the United Kingdom and do my thing, and then return to my job in a year's

time. For me, the Queen of Attachments, this solution was ideal. It meant that I didn't have to break my ties with the company and that I would have guaranteed employment when I returned. Above all, it meant that I wouldn't have to undertake any make-or-break decisions just yet.

So that was how my life began to change even without me looking for it. Up until this point, I never really had to plan what was going to happen next. It all seemed like a logical progression: from year to year at school; from school to university; from year to year at university; from university to a job which seemed an obvious step for someone with multiple interests and abilities. I would have left it at that for the time being, if my boyfriend hadn't done that which many ideal partners do: act as the direct opposite to some of my most deep-seated characteristics, and rock my very stable boat. I didn't really think beyond the year in London, since the company's 'leave of absence' gave me the sacred right to return.

So I went along with this next unexpected, yet logical, turn in my tide, and set off for the distant shores of the Mud Island.

Enter the Quarterlife Crisis

Looking back, I think that this move to the UK was in fact the birth of my Quarterlife Crisis, although I didn't know it at the time. The Quarterlife Crisis is a condition that thrives on a change in the status quo. Open the door to opportunity, and the big QC comes waltzing through the door. I had always lived a relatively sheltered life, at least with respect to the number of big decisions I'd had to make. So changing tack and doing something I never before would have dreamed of doing before, certainly shifted the foundations and loosened a few stones. But for the time being, I was skipping down this next path, eyes peeled for adventure and ready to try something new.

[for a crisis]

In my first few weeks as a Londoner, I challenged my own concept of myself so many times that I was beginning to forget what I looked like. Soon enough, though, I was visited by the old drive to be doing, achieving, participating. And it wasn't just me; in a city such as this one, people's lives appeared to revolve around their work. Certainly, the drive to earn money is fierce since London is an extremely expensive place to live and is best optimised on a decent budget. I had shaken my roots considerably during this time and felt so new and inexperienced, that I was starting to miss that sense of certainty and self-confidence that comes with doing something you know you can do. So I presented myself to the numerous recruitment agents who clog the arteries of the employment world, and began the search for a job.

It was tempting to slip back into the types of roles to which I had become accustomed in my job at home. They were non-threatening, available, and sufficiently part of my past life to help me feel secure. But something pressed on the release catch of my adventurer's spirit and I knew I should look for something different: this was a new life, where very few people knew me – why not take a chance? But 'risk-averse' should have been my middle name; and I am my own biggest critic. I wasn't ready to test the waters of Quarterlife without a flotation device. So I chose the middle ground. I opted for a different kind of consulting work in an entirely new environment: a very small and highly creative company which was still in its infancy and had a long way to grow. The work had a different focus from my previous job, but still held enough of a consulting flavour to soothe my apprehensive taste buds. I would be challenged, without being terrified.

So life as a real Londoner began in earnest. I eased into it quite happily, encountering only a few culture shocks along the way and learning quickly that I would soon become an outcast if I kept up my annoyance of English pubs. I made great friends at work and relished the closeness of my friends from home, who were also fighting their own private battles to assimilate into this new way of being. Ex-pats in London tend to stick together, which inevitably mitigates the full onslaught of being a foreigner, but I made sure to mix in multiple circles. I am a stickler for habit, so I quickly inserted strict regularities into my daily existence and approached my work (and my life) in much the same way as I had done in the past. I soon began to enjoy a sense of accomplishment in that I was successfully integrating into a new city, and had managed to find a flat and a job. I began to achieve at work and seemed to gain the respect of my colleagues, even if they did think I was strange for throwing open the blinds and windows every time there was a hint of sunlight. As I had always done, I quickly smoothed over any uncertainties in my life's path and put a familiar flow in their place. Life was sweet.

We travelled as often as we could within the UK and Europe and tried to make the most of living in the world's epicentre. I hardly thought about the future and the fact that this situation was temporary; I fixed myself in the present and looked no further.

Just when I was getting comfortable...

So it was through my future-protective glasses that I looked at Richard incredulously, one afternoon about a year after arriving in London and shortly after a trip home to Cape Town during the Christmas break, when he suggested that we get away for the weekend.

'But we've just gotten back from being away,' I said, suddenly exhausted at the thought of another suitcase.

'But it's our six-year anniversary and we should celebrate. How about we just head to that little town called Bath? It's only a few hours' drive from here.'

I couldn't argue with that. 'OK fine. You do the bookings.' That should stump him.

See what a sucker for routine I am? I'd even give up a weekend away in an historic destination just to have my regular breakfast and sleep on my own mattress.

Friday afternoon, after work, Richard picked me up at the train station and off we went to Bath. Having committed to the trip, I was now pretty pleased that we were going away, and I was soon belting out show tunes and car songs to my heart's content. But the trip took longer than we had expected and by the time we reached our destination B&B, it was way past the receptionist's bedtime. I was tired. It had been a long week and I was starting to feel sick from the excessive amounts of junk food that I regard as my entitlement on a road trip. So I certainly wasn't prepared for what happened next.

Richard has a problem being serious. He has as relaxed a view on life as any person I've ever met and smiling is how he rests his face. So I knew something was up when he sat down next to me once we had unpacked our bags and shaken the traveller's dust from our coats. He wasn't smiling now. His face was blank and his whole demeanour was poised to spring. He ignored my efforts at silly jokes and playful tickles. And I knew beyond a shadow of a doubt that this was it.

I won't go into the gory (but delicious) details of exactly how Richard proposed marriage to me. I will tell you, though, that the proposal was a mixture of caramelised poetry and little drops of heaven-speak. In my characteristic stance of surprise, I shrieked, clapped my hand over my mouth, and burst into tears. Richard stoically presented me with a £5.50, 14-day-money-back-guarantee ring in lieu of any precious stones for the time being, and promptly collapsed from nervous tension. I stayed awake all night, reliving the moment, mouthing the word 'engaged', and trying to get the cubic zirconium to catch the light of the street lamps. What a night! I barely saw Bath that weekend, and our friends in London insisted we return to the city the next night to celebrate with them. We still have the scrap of paper with the name of some random guy we met while we were out partying; it reads

'Congratulations! From Keith Jones – the first stranger you told about your engage-ment'. And so, just like that, I became a fiancée. I didn't know, nor did I worry too much, whether things would have to change to suit my new title. I was content with my spot on Cloud 9 and, once we'd decided to get married in a year's time, intended to stay there for a good long while.

Decision time

As if that wasn't enough change for one year, we also had to face the reality that our work visas would expire soon and we would either have to apply to stay permanently, or move on. I couldn't bear to think about choosing where to live next – whether we should stay in London permanently, go back to South Africa or move to a new destination. Before I could get too bogged down in all of this, Richard reminded me that our initial plan had been to come to London for enough time to earn some money with which we could then travel for an extended period. I had almost forgotten that the 'goal' of London was to travel but, when I thought about travelling for a few months, I worried about the break in our lives. Wouldn't we lose out on valuable career-building time if we gave it all up for the spirit of adventure? Wouldn't I freak out if I weren't progressing, achieving, moving forward? At the same time, though, this was probably the ideal time in my life to do something wild and wonderful. How many people would kill for the chance to have a long holiday to see the world and gain the growth and experience that can only come from travel? In fact, the more I thought about it, the more I became convinced that this was a once-in-a-lifetime opportunity, and that I would really regret not doing it now, at this time in my life when I had few commitments, lots of energy and enough guts to rough it in the big wide world. I was torn in this decision to travel or not, but in the end I just decided that it was only six months of my life and I might never get the chance again – at least not until retirement age, at which point I might not rel-ish leaving the comfort of my rocking chair.

Of course, I had to contend with the issue of the leave of absence. I laboured over how to explain my decision to the firm and spent so many sleepless nights feeling bad about it that I almost changed my mind for the sake of maintaining the status quo. I called my manager back at my old job in South Africa and explained the situation. But the response was hardly what I'd expected. The company insisted that I extend my leave of absence for another year as they fully respected the wanderlust I was experiencing. My job would be waiting for me if and when I returned home in a year's time. As for my job in London, well, leaving was harder than I expected it to be, but I had realised by this stage that the British system of endless rainfall, traffic and subterranean travel didn't suit my surfer-boy fiancé (see I'm getting used to the word), and the chance of returning to London was slight.

The next few months were spent planning our travels: a month back home in Cape Town to plan the wedding; about four months travelling in Asia and the Far East; and then a month back home again just before the wedding to tie up loose ends and annoy our mothers. Our wedding, of course, was the subject of endless discussions and by the time we left London, we had a 20 page document outlining every last detail for the event. (See my touch anywhere in this?!) I was content. I had successfully avoided making any lasting decisions and was poised on the brink of another real adventure.

The allure of travel

So that's how I came to be standing on the platform of a train bound for Irkutsk, Siberia, bearing precious few of my worldly possessions on my back, trying to memorise the Russian words for 'I'm a vegetarian'. Oh, the subject of our travels is enough for an entire book on its own, but let's skip to the moment of truth.

Four months, 32 rolls of film and a severe tan later, I found myself on the happy isle of Koh Lanta, my favourite spot on our Thai travels and the place that has my very own bum-print deeply embedded in its endless stretch of perfect beach. Aside from checking in regularly with my mom about wedding preparations and dreaming about the day, I hadn't really thought about going back home – it all seemed so far away still. But as I lay one day watching the tiny crabs roll miniscule balls of sand, I was suddenly struck by the fact that we only had two weeks to go before leaving our travels behind.

In the grand scheme of four months, two weeks is nothing! I couldn't wait for my wedding day, but I surely did not want to return to reality. Heck, I didn't even know what reality was any more. It certainly wasn't life at home in Cape Town: I had taken a leave of absence, sold my car and cancelled all debit orders before we left for London. My ties to home were tenuous – my biggest commitment there was the booking for the wedding venue. Did I even want to go back and live there? Was I sure that I wanted to go back to my old job? Our time in London and these months of carefree travel had changed my own definition of myself so dramatically that I was having trouble picturing my old life. I had gotten used to living without the rules and strict characterisation that I had taken comfort in before. I was now a chilled-out traveller chick, citizen of the world and lady of leisure. I knew I couldn't live like this forever but did I know what I wanted to go back to?

Who and what am I?
And just like that – lazing on my lilo in the Gulf of Thailand, watermelon milkshake close at hand and only 14 days of bronzing to go – it hit me: aside from the wedding, the future was unclear. Other than knowing who I was to spend the rest of my life with (at least I had that one sorted out – it could have been worse!), I had no idea of the nature of my days to come. I had a leave of absence, but no obligation to return to work. I was qualified – but for what? I was dedicated – but to what?

What was I? What would I become? How would I earn a living? One of the first things that people would ask when we met them was 'What do you do?' and I would lazily tell them that I was a management consultant. But was I really, deep down inside?

Sometimes, when people asked that same-old question, Richard and I would pretend to be something exotic: like a wildlife photographer and travel journalist; or an archaeologist and a news reporter; or a magician and a porn star (well, not really, but let's just say…). It was fun to play around like that, but it got me wondering whether I was content enough with what I had been doing to carry on doing it. The more I thought about how uncertain the future was, the faster I drank my watermelon milkshake and the less I wanted to go home. So I just stopped… thinking about the future, that is. I just didn't allow my thoughts to stroll any further than the 30th December – my wedding date, a month and a half away. I dreamed wedding dreams and woke up to spend the days converting them into reality. I found the most obscure stones to overturn, just so that I wouldn't have to think about anything else. I was determined that the wedding was going to be the event of my lifetime – of everyone's lifetime – and no detail would go un-obsessed about. I had fun. No doubt about that. In fact, I had so much fun consuming myself with wedding stuff that I began to count the seconds until I could return to Cape Town and really get stuck into the preparations. I certainly wasn't about to let life, or Quarterlife, get in the way.

As they say, hindsight is 20/20, and I now realise that all this happy-go-lucky flitting around the world was merely feeding the Quarterlife Crisis that my move to London had unleashed. Having jolted myself out of complacency and the regularity of moving from one pre-determined life phase to another, I had gone on to stoke the glowing embers of a phenomenon that feeds on change and uncertainty. All these adventures in the wide world, undertaken with no real end point in mind, while entirely worthwhile and completely irreplaceable as far as life experience goes, were also nice chunks of protein, fattening the Quarterlife monster and making it grow. I was hardly ready to shake hands with my crisis and welcome it in. Far from it. I was having much too much fun ignoring its rapidly expanding girth and was content to simply buy bigger sizes for it to wear. I knew that the future lay undetermined ahead of me, filled with multiple possibilities and numerous decisions, but I wanted to just press the 'snooze' button on it for now. So I rolled over, and went back to sleep – dreaming of my wedding day as if it were the end of time itself.

THE HONEYMOON [phase]

Few things in life turn out just the way you've planned or hoped. My wedding day was such an exception. The month at home after our travels to organise and obsess over the wedding was as much fun, and as hectic, as I'd imagined. I surprised even myself by resisting the temptation to become a hysterical bride and by keeping pretty calm throughout the pre-wedding onslaught. It was an over-whelmingly happy time and, above all, I felt really fortunate. During that month, I counted the days to the wedding as if each one were a jewel in a crown; they were satiated moments, during which life revolved around the target date and stopped right there – anything beyond it was beside the point.

The day dawned bright and early for me, and by 10am the house was a hive of activity. The next few hours flew past and I had to keep reminding myself to 'take a moment', to concentrate on the enormity and uniqueness of the day and to try not to let it race by too quickly. It's a great technique that: it helps to ground you in the present and reminds you to take in the details before they become lost in the big picture.

So we floated down the aisle, chiffon and silk moving slowly in what our guests described as a caravan of colour. When I finally faced Richard under the bridal canopy, outside, beneath the watchful eye of Table Mountain, it was the culmination of moments, days, months of dreaming. In an admittedly clichéd, yet blissfully authentic move, the strong wind, which had blown since the morning, released its grip for a while and every part of me sang. We were surely the first couple on earth to ever get married; we were surely the first couple on earth.

I have always wondered how most brides manage to keep such genuine-looking smiles on their faces throughout the wedding. There's really no choice – your mouth just seems to creep upwards without even really trying. And thank goodness for those photos which show the details, because much of the night blends into a happy kaleidoscope of dancing, well-wishing and public displays of affection. Some parts of it, though, I remember with crystal clarity: leaving the bridal canopy on Richard's arm, our multicoloured bridal party leading the way; my first view of the hall which had been transformed into a magical wooded fairyland of leaves and light; our first dance, during which every person in the room seemed to disappear, leaving only my new husband as if spotlighted in my consciousness; the changing lights reflected on the domed ceiling of the hall – purples into pinks into greens and blues, evolving with the movement of the night; my wedding speech, during which I took the chance to say, in public, those things that you never take the time to say in private; the bitter-sweet end of the night, when saying goodbye to friends who had come from so far meant not seeing them again for ages; and my final glance back at the place that had been the scene of my changing life, shimmering lights still glazing the mountainside and the strains of the quartet still wafting over the sleeping city.

The Quarterlife Crisis can wait

Of course, amidst the perfection of it all, I also clearly remember my growing aware-ness that this was the night I'd been planning for so long; everything beyond today had ceased to exist in the build-up to the wedding. Yet now, here we were, on the brink of a day – in fact, a future – which was entirely unclear. I was now a 'Mrs', but didn't really understand how that was going to change my life; I was effectively unemployed (although the leave of absence still applied), but didn't really know what work I wanted to do; I had come home for the wedding, but didn't really know if this was where we were going to stay; I was old enough to get married, but didn't really feel the merit of enough age or experience to face this great big void of uncertainty. For a few brief moments on this otherwise faultless night, I came to understand that Quarterlife was where I stood and its associated Crisis was what I faced. I had neither the time nor the inclination to contemplate it further, but I knew that I couldn't avoid it forever. We had played a convenient game of cat and mouse over the past year or so, but it had started to catch up with me and getting away would be difficult. For now, however, I had guests to attend to, a husband to gaze at and make-up to fix. Quarterlife would have to wait.

I spent the next couple of days in a post-wedding reverie. Everyone seemed to have had an absolute ball, and the detail and effort that went into the planning weren't lost on a soul. I didn't want to let go of my elation, so I used the wedding photos, gifts and still-blooming flowers to stretch out wedding fever.

Richard had been planning a surprise honeymoon – I knew nothing of the destination or even the duration, only that we would be leaving about ten days after the wedding. I couldn't wait for the honeymoon, but I was really happy about having some extra time at home to ride the post-wedding wave. But three days after the event, I hit an all-time

low. I started to feel really down; even the presence of my favourite people and the prospect of a few hidden wedding gifts couldn't lighten my load. I was grateful for my new husband, but completely depressed that the wedding was over. This occasion that I had looked forward to for so long, that I had dedicated more time, energy and creativity to than any project in my life... this *pièce de resistance* of a lifetime, was over. I felt flat. I wanted to get married again – to the same man, of course, and in the same way. In fact, I wanted to have the whole engagement year back. People sympathised with my misery, but couldn't really understand. And I felt selfish for feeling so depressed when everything had turned out so well. But I couldn't shake off the dejection.

The arrival of the wedding video did lots to lift my spirits, and we watched it far too many times. But during the course of these few days, during the highs and the lows, I had the niggling sensation that there was something unchecked on my to-do list. All the questions about my future that had surfaced, however briefly, on my wedding day, had not been resolved, and I knew that I hadn't given them the attention they were demanding. Of course the future is far too enormous a subject to go unresolved for very long, but procrastination is the opiate of the lazy, and I was head sloth as far as this issue was concerned. So I hauled out the old broomstick and brushed my burgeoning Quarterlife Crisis firmly under the rug again, content to let my honeymoon take centre stage for now.

The question of location

Packing, of course, was a problem. I had no idea where we were going. Richard said to pack for any eventuality, so my luggage included bikinis, scarves, suntan lotion and thermal underwear. I knew we were starting in the United States since we had been invited, by our various siblings, to 'check it out' as far as potential living arrangements were concerned: all our siblings are now residents of the US and were keen that we should come over and join them. Being open to all options at this stage, we agreed to do a reconnaissance trip there before the surprise honeymoon. So we set off for midwinter in North America and a whirlwind trip of possible cities to call 'home' when we eventually settled down. I was focused on the trip at the end of the trip, so I'm not sure that I gave adequate attention to the candidates for 'where to next?'. Also, I didn't really feel like concentrating on a decision as huge as our future residence. Home, as in South Africa, was still a happy place for me – in fact, its familiarity had become even more attractive since I'd been away for so long – so the 'America decision', as it came to be known, felt premature. Of course, it was also competing with the heavyweight 'Australia decision' which had become an option on our visit to the Land of Oz during our pre-wedding travels. Hell, why not throw Canada, Europe and the UK into the bag while we're at it? Anyway, I went along with the sightseeing, concentrating on the fun of the excursion rather than the pending decisions.

Our flight to Miami was meant to be a surprise, but despite plugging my fingers in my ears, I overheard the check-in agent confirming the destination with Richard. Never mind – Richard had managed to keep it a surprise all this time. He told me that he had hired a house on the beach and that we were going to spend the next week being waited on hand and foot and getting our tans going again. Awesome! As it turns out, the beach house Richard had hired turned out to be a huge cruise ship – a veritable floating city docked in the Miami harbour and elegantly waiting to take us to four exotic destinations in the Caribbean. Now that's a surprise!

The tenacious persistence of Quarterlife

After a crazy wedding month, it was good to have the time to ourselves. At times, though, something nagged in the background. I would be soaking up the sun in the Roman Baths section of the boat, sipping a glass of the champagne that my brother and sister had sent to our cabin before our departure. Thinking of them would bring the US to the forefront of my mind and I would be reminded of the possibility of us moving there after our honeymoon. Of course, that would make me think of all the other choices regarding where to live, setting up a spiralling internal debate as to whether I was ready to leave home again and, if so, where would I go to? A waiter carrying strawberry daiquiris and blessed with impeccable timing would stir me out of my reverie, but not before my subconscious mind had had a chance to pull at the threads of my perfect holiday. On another occasion, I would be strolling along the streets of Ochos Rios, Jamaica, yelling 'Hey mon, no problem, Mon' to unassuming passers-by, when some taxi driver would offer to take Richard and his 'Missus' on a tour. I still hadn't come to terms with the fact that I was now a wife, and I certainly couldn't yet call myself by anything other than the name I'd always known. That, of course, would start me wondering about how things in our relationship, and in my life, were going to change with my new identity as Richard's wife, which in turn would start me questioning what my old identity had been and what I was going to do with my life from now on. A noisy procession celebrating Bob Marley's birthday would jolt me back to the present, but not before the ghost of the Quarterlife Crisis had started a slow leak. Even a lazy meal at the all-you-can-eat buffet was not safe from such intrusions. I would be innocently trying to choose between a muffin and a bagel, when the analogy would creep into my head: my past life was like the muffin – dense, defined, whole – while my future life was like the bagel – generally nice and round but with a hole in the middle. If I chose the bagel, I would have to work out how to plug the hollow of indecision. Such were the trials of breakfast time.

Above all, though, this was my honeymoon and I was determined to enjoy it as one of those life experiences that I am unlikely to have ever again. At the back of my mind I knew that, once the honeymoon was over and we returned home, I would have to face all these worrying questions. And there would be no cocktails or Rastafarians to distract me.

So I made the most of the sheer decadence of a cruise holiday, and every time the Quarterlife Crisis twitched, I would eat another bagel, take another book out of the ship's library, or slot a token into one more arcade game.

I probably wouldn't have been so calm about everything if I had realised quite how much there was to deal with when I got home. But I see now that my slump after the wedding and my uncomfortable musings during the honeymoon were part of the same thing: a slow settling of the Quarterlife Crisis. I had assumed that my postnuptial low was simply part of the anticlimax that almost always follows a big event. But now I think it was more than that: it was the anxiety of a crisis that could not be contained for much longer; it was the apprehension of having to make some major life changes without the comfort of childhood predictability – I must be such a 'big girl' now that I was married, yet life seemed more uncertain than ever before; it was the fear of the unknown that lay beyond the safety net of my wedding day.

The honeymoon itself had been my last fling within a relatively risk-free life in which convention had laid out comfortable boundaries and responsibility was more my parents' than my own. But the honeymoon marked the end of that and the beginning of a future I hadn't wanted to imagine, despite how exciting or different or opportunity-filled it might be. Childhood was a thing of the past and true adulthood beckoned. Uh oh1

We spent our last day on board the honeymoon boat quietly watching Miami draw closer. I fiddled with my wedding band, almost like checking to make sure it was still there. Coming back to shore was like waking from a dream, one that had gone on for years of my life during which I had stirred awake a few times, but mostly just to reconnect with the world for a moment before floating back into a blissful slumber. This time, though, the lights were shining brightly in my eyes and the coffee was ready and waiting. It had been an unforgettable trip but it was time to go home.

FACING [the music]

We returned to Cape Town because that was home – and home seemed like the best place to tackle what I sensed would be a formative time in my adult life. It's always good to come back to base now and then, particularly when you need to muster all your resources for your next sortie into the unknown.

Landing at Cape Town International Airport was strange. Usually, I felt that unbridled patriotic need to break into the national anthem as the plane banked over Table Mountain. This time, though, both Richard and I were quiet and thoughtful. There was a sense of resignation, of knowing that there were no more ways to stall the inevitable. It was showtime, and reality was in the hot seat.

My mother fetched us from the airport and we drove through streets still waking to the end of summer. Thankfully, we had kept our old apartment during the two years that we'd been away, and my mom dropped us off there now to unpack and get settled. I didn't quite know what to do with myself once she had left. Endless days stretched out in front of me and I would have to mould them to take on a form I couldn't even identify. We were back, but I felt a million miles away.

Sorting through life

To get myself going, I started with the relatively easy task of sorting clothes and unpacking boxes stacked in our apartment. It was during this sorting session which was, I suppose, a mental clearing in some senses as well, that I paged through a book I had read towards the end of our time in London. In it, I found my bookmark – an article that I had torn out of a newspaper. It was a small filler column, of the type that lurks on the edge of busy pages, with no listed author and a punchy title. It was all about this relatively undefined but widespread condition called the 'Quarterlife Crisis'. I remembered reading the article during a typical crushed morning on the London Underground on the way to work and, finding it intriguing, had torn it out and put it to the grandiose task of being my latest bookmark. In fact, it was this article that had first introduced me to the idea that there even was such a thing as the Quarterlife Crisis, but it took some months before I was ready to contemplate the concept fully and, in so doing, face my own.

I stared at the article and recalled the flash of recognition that had pierced me when I read it for the first time. All this uncertainty about my future, all the expectations I had of myself and the ones I thought everyone else had of me, all my questions about where to live and what to do and who to be... there was a name for it all! And it's not as if it was identified by some reclusive scientist examining a near-extinct tribe in deepest, darkest Africa; this is a condition as common to Quarterlifers as acne is to teenagers.

Something clicked that day as I stood among piles of clothes, books and arbitrary kitchen utensils. Before then, I hadn't been ready to face the reality of the future and the magnitude of issues I felt awaited me. It was almost like going to the store to buy bread; when you get there, you find that you must choose between white bread, brown bread, wholewheat, rye, seed loaf, thick slice, thin slice, low-calorie, French, olive, herb bread... until eventually, you are so fed up with all the alternatives that you turn around and walk out, deciding that you'd rather starve. I hadn't felt like making choices up to now and had held out on the challenges as far as possible. Avoidance *par excellence*, I'd say. But it's difficult to do that for very long, particularly for someone like me who dislikes surprises (unless they are of the precious stone variety), preferring to know where she's going and how she's going to get there. I had relinquished control of my surroundings to some extent, and had actually quite enjoyed the relative recklessness, but it couldn't go on forever. It wasn't in my nature not to know.

The here and now

As it became more and more apparent that 'the future was now' and I'd have to face facts, I started to feel panicky. I woke up in the mornings with a nervous apprehension, not knowing what to expect from the day. I was still on a leave of absence, so my time was free. But I wasn't on holiday any longer and I missed the structure of my past life. My avoidance of the Quarterlife Crisis had been the best defence mechanism for warding off the anxiety that is often associated with the condition. But now my guard was down and I felt worried. I drank endless cups of coffee and slept at the oddest daylight hours. I grew quiet, refusing to discuss my plans with anyone – mainly because I didn't know what those plans were. I was too afraid to admit that I hadn't defined my next steps. I had been head girl of my school, chair-person of university organisations, a supposedly organised, goal-directed, ambitious individual who always, always had the answers. How could I confess to not knowing what I wanted to do or where I wanted to be? I was married – but so what? Just because you start ticking the 'Mrs' box on questionnaires and doctors' forms, doesn't mean you suddenly have your life all planned out. And I was afraid of committing to any big decisions in case they turned out to be the wrong ones, or in case I wasn't able to succeed at them in the way I had always achieved in the past.

The soap opera moment technique

Over the next few weeks, I worked myself into a state of nervous and unproductive tension. I tried to look at the situation objectively and to draw on the tried and tested skills that had stood me in such good stead in the past. For as long as I can remember, I have always adopted some personal, useful techniques to help me get through stress. One of these, I called my 'soap opera moments'. Let me explain. Through school and university, the most overtly stressful times were during exams. Everyone always dreaded midyears and finals and I, being one who took her studies really seriously, was a real stress-ball during those periods. To help me get through exam-time, I would choose things to look forward to, and would focus on those whenever the pressure of exams got me down. I would build these beacons of light into my life as short-, medium- and long-term goals. Short-term goals were used on a daily basis, and they inevitably included looking forward to my regular soap-opera episode of the 'Bold & the Beautiful', which, like clockwork at 6:00pm every day, would give me a welcome break from studying. Medium-term goals were used on a weekly basis. So they might include a lunch arrangement with a friend, or a hair appointment, which I would build into my study schedule to help get my mind off stress. Long-term goals were always reserved for the end of exams: the holiday I had planned or a great book I was dying to read. All these goals, collectively called soap-opera moments, would help me get through the stress and tedium of exams by encouraging me to focus on the lights at the end of the tunnel.

So now, during this Quarterlife stress, I tried to do the same thing. I was sorely tempted to use my leave of absence end date as my soap-opera moment, but I was no longer entirely sure that consulting was the right route. I questioned the lifestyle and didn't feel convinced that that was really my life's ambition. This crisis was an excuse to re-evaluate. It would have been warm and comfortable to slot back into that work life I had known, and goodness knows it would have alleviated at least one of the big stressors, but did that necessarily mean it was the right choice? Of course, the thought of sifting through the alternatives was also daunting. If only I had an overriding dream or a passion that would guide me, inexorably, towards it. I've always had so many interests; why didn't one of them grab me now?

The enlightenment technique

It seemed that even effective soap-opera moments were eluding me. So I turned to the next weapon in my arsenal of stress beaters – 'enlightenment'. I generally prefer to view life from an academic, intellectual point of view. I always take time to work things out in my head first, rationalising and analysing to my heart's content. Intellectualising usually helps me deal with pressure because I feel I at least understand my issues and have some sensation of 'seeing the light'. So I decided to try and understand my Quarterlife Crisis. Rather than shunning it, I thought it might be worthwhile to get to grips with it all: myself, my situation, my choices, and my future options. Life felt like a bit of a quagmire – it would do me well to sift through it.

I started by trying to find out as much as I could about the Quarterlife Crisis. As it happens, there isn't all that much out there, but what I did find was interesting, such as a book entitled 'Quarterlife Crisis. How to get your head round life in your twenties' by Alexandra Robbins and Abby Wilner (Bloomsbury). But that wasn't enough. I also started opening my eyes and ears, talking with friends, acquaintances and any Quarterlifer who was prepared to give me a minute, about what was happening in their lives. Remarkably, it appeared that scores of people – even those I thought I had known well and whom I had envied for how settled they seemed – were going through many of the same things that I was. The difficulty in making choices about where to live, what career to choose, how to live your life, when to make what decisions… was more common than I had realised and I learned a fortune from the people who shared their stories. I also found willing narrators in the parents and friends of Quarterlifers who, when I mentioned the concept, nodded their heads in agreement and told me what they, too, had observed. Certainly, the more I concentrated on the Quarterlife Crisis, the more I began to define my own situation and clarify my own experiences.

Defining the Quarterlife Crisis

The Quarterlife Crisis' can be generally defined as that unique crisis of modern twenty- and thirty somethings who are faced with an overwhelming number of choices and expectations regarding their futures. It typically strikes when Quarterlifers are making their transition from college or university to the big wide world of true adults. It can take a while to play itself out, particularly since modern Quarterlifers have numerous options during this transition phase: you can start building a single career, or try different jobs; you can travel, or study further, or start a family. Talking to others, I've found that the crisis sometimes becomes apparent (again or for the first time) at other key transitional phases in the twenties and thirties, such as moving on from your first job, or returning from a year's travel, or getting married. Whatever the circumstances, the Quarterlife Crisis is marked by a period of intense change which often causes anxiety about your current and future states.

One thing that makes the Quarterlife Crisis so difficult is the feeling of losing control: you emerge from an existence where life was largely predictable to a situation of instability and changeability. For instance, in the academic environment, you always knew what you had to do in order to progress or achieve: courses were structured, feedback was organised around tests or exams, and advancement was a simple matter of pass or fail. If you were good at sports, you went to practice and tried out for the team. If you liked to sing, you joined the choir. But when you enter the world at large, you find that the choices are numerous, and the consequences of those choices are a lot more serious. You start having to rely on yourself a great deal more than ever before, and it's difficult to know when you are on the right track. No-one hands out grades or gold stars anymore and paying the bills isn't half as much fun as you thought it would be. Topping it all, you expect certain things of yourself based on your previous life and you sense that society has expectations, too. But you're not sure what you have to do to meet them.

The new generation

The Quarterlife Crisis is unique because it was heralded by a generation of people who came of age during the technology boom, a time when 25-year olds were making millions off new generation companies. At the same time, computer expertise, often perceived as the domain of the young, became the skill *du jour*. One minute your next-door neighbour was graduating, and the next he was parading around in a BMW convertible with his secretary running to keep up with his dictation. Suddenly, everyone else seems to have achieved so much more than you have, while you're still trying to figure out what to have for lunch. But the reality is

that they fell as high as they flew in the technology boom. Many made millions, but many lost millions too. Of course, this is an important fact, largely overlooked by often-despondent Quarterlifers who still question why they don't yet have a corner office. The majority of us, however, are ordinary people with what has become a common dilemma. We have developed almost unrealistic expectations of ourselves, and feel like failures when those expectations haven't been achieved by the ripe old age of twenty-something.

The generations before us did not experience the same degree of choice or flux. Certainly, there are far more opportunities and alternatives these days, a fact that our parents often regard as a blessing rather than a curse. How often have you heard: 'You've got your whole life ahead of you and you can be anything you want to be. You're very lucky!', while at the same time you're thinking, 'I wish things were simpler and clearer; having so many choices just makes everything that much more complicated.'

Take the choice of where to live, for one. When my grandmother moved to this country from eastern Europe 73 years ago, it took her one week by train to London, and three weeks by boat from London to Cape Town. And it was no luxury travel either. With that type of journey to contend with, she certainly wasn't moving anywhere else once she had laid down her roots here! Today, you can do the same trip in about 15 hours by airplane and, as every mother says, 'the world is your oyster'. With some effort, you can live almost anywhere in the world. But is that such a good thing? Yes, the world is a far smaller place, and we are fortunate to have relatively easy access to it, but that just makes it so much more difficult to choose a place to settle – particularly since families and friends are often spread all over the place. So Quarterlifers, about to take up the more 'established' phase of their lives, need now add the consideration of where to live to the host of other questions they face.

Choosing a home, and a job, and a partner, and a course in life is all very 'real'. Certainly, the Quarterlife Crisis hinges on a growing awareness of your concerns as an adult, and of a sense that the decisions you make now are somehow more loaded than ever before. Many Quarterlifers, having removed their blinkers, are often swamped by the unexpected force of the modern world. Some suffer real panic and depression, overwhelmed by feeling helpless, uncertain and afraid.

Almost all decline to talk about it with others, either not recognising the nature of their dilemma or embarrassed to admit that they are struggling with a time that is supposed to be brimming with opportunity and prospects. Most Quarterlifers feel that they are the only people on earth who are experiencing such indecision and insecurity – certainly the Quarterlifers I approached were amazed to think that others were encountering similar predicaments and warmed to the discussion in the same way that you greet an old friend in an unexpected place.

A widespread condition

The Quarterlife Crisis has cloaked itself in mystery: you don't expect it, so you feel uncomfortable with it, so you keep quiet about it, so you don't take comfort in knowing that others have it, so you battle it out alone, so professionals don't analyse it, so there's nothing on the self-help shelves when you try to solve it. That's why it's a crisis: because it feels like there are no answers to the myriad questions you have; because you try and go it alone while so many others have been there, will be there, and could benefit from your experience; because the world expects more of you than it ever has; because you can swing from choice to choice and still have a bagful waiting to be discovered; because 30 is not too young to retire; and because you realise that life is a couple of sandwiches short of a picnic.

You know how when you hear a new word and look it up in the dictionary, it then seems to appear everywhere? That was how it was for me once I re-read that article about the Quarterlife Crisis and began to unravel its mysteries – suddenly, every person between the ages of 20 to 35 seemed to be going through the crisis, has gone through it in the past, or has identified some element of it in themselves. And as for me – every sentence I read or heard about the Quarterlife Crisis seemed to apply to me in some way. The more I realised how commonplace it was, the less alone I felt, and this sense of solidarity with my peers took the edge off my anxiety. Of course, every person is unique, which makes every crisis unique, too: not everyone gets depressed or panicky; not everyone experiences all parts of it; and not every Quarterlifer goes through such a crisis. But there is a basic footprint that the Quarterlife Crisis treads and the more we study it, the more people acknowledge it, the closer we'll get to knowing its shoe size.

The compartmentalisation technique

Well, it had been fun getting to know my Quarterlife Crisis, but I was no closer to solving it. Of course, recognition and understanding are always the first steps to resolution – hence the much publicised methodology of Alcoholics Anonymous, where the first words out of a recovering alcoholic's mouth are 'I am so-and-so and I'm an alcoholic'. Admitting to your condition is part of the battle won. OK, so then, 'My name is Joanne and I'm having a Quarterlife Crisis.' Now what? Well, here I had to rely on my personal cache of stress busters again – yes, the very same one that had yielded soap-opera moments and my proclivity for thinking that a bubble bath will solve my troubles.

Now I turned to what I call 'Compartmentalisation'. Inevitably, issues in your life are not isolated – they are intimately connected with other concerns and it sometimes becomes difficult to see the wood for the trees. I always find it useful to divide things up into segments, and then deal with them one at a time. That way, by eliminating the volume of critical mass, problems seem less daunting and can be managed in their own time, in their own way.

So I looked at the various components of my Quarterlife Crisis and found patterns that could be largely consolidated into the following compartments:

The career crisis: the dilemma of choosing a job, profession or vocation.
The dream crisis: the dilemma of finding your life's passion.
The location crisis: the dilemma of where to live.
The age crisis: the dilemma of when to do what, and feeling simultaneously 'old' and 'young'.
The identity crisis: the dilemma of self-definition.

Each one is a crisis in itself and, as if they aren't enough to deal with individually, they often tend to hit you all at once in the Quarterlife Crisis. That's why the emotions of Quarterlife are critical, too, since the crisis is attended by its own range of ups and downs. But to manage the crisis effectively, I felt it was vital that these components be given their own space for consideration. After all, why should only chocolate bars come in bite-size chunks?

WHAT SHOULD I DO? [the career crisis]

My Quarterlife Crisis was kick-started by the question of which career to choose. Although many aspects of Quarterlife vied with each other for my attention, the question of career was probably the one with the longest life span. It all started at the end of my university studies, when I had completed my degree and faced a variety of professional paths. I began to understand that the very fact that I had an education opened multiple doors for me, not simply the ones to which I had limited my studies. Obviously, a particular course tends to lead people in a specific direction (for example, only those who study medicine can ever become doctors), but it doesn't always mean that they are confined to that path (not all those who obtain medical degrees necessarily do become doctors). Now, more than ever before, the world has opened its doors to a person's potential rather than his or her qualification or proven ability. Hence the possibility that I could apply for a job in management consulting with a humanities degree in clinical psychology. So the dilemma of what job or profession to choose becomes apparent with the sheer number of possibilities available, particularly to people who have a tertiary education.

For me, the chance to work in the business world was daunting and unexpected, but I relished the possibility of broadening my horizons in that way. I also started to see that much of what I had to learn could quite reasonably be done on the job rather than in the classroom – as long as I had the drive, the enthusiasm and the ability to learn. I would be fine without the B.Comm, at least for the time being. The thought that I was trying something new, while also building a socially respectable career, lessened the crisis potential when I left university. I wasn't thinking about whether I wanted to do this forever or if this would be my life's work. All I knew was that to continue with psychology would require further study, and preferably some real-life experience, before committing to the master's degree. So I staved off the real onset of my career crisis by jumping into my next step – it wasn't hard to do, since society approved of this job choice and I knew that the experience would be worthwhile, no matter how things might turn out. I suppose that is something of a luxury, too – the ability to do things without really worrying about the repercussions – and it is part of what complicates Quarterlife. Quarterlifers aren't yet bound by too many responsibilities and your decisions generally affect only yourself. As a result, the scope of opportunity broadens even further – you're young and able, very little is irreparable. Still, that is not to say that you don't worry about your decisions, since they and their potential consequences seem more serious than ever before

Of course, things became more confused when I took a leave of absence from my job. Although I had decided to spend the following year in London, I left the question of career choice open. Life at my consulting company was structured and formalised: promotion and career advancement were clearly mapped out and achievable according to fixed criteria. Whilst the consulting lifestyle was often unsteady, with projects changing regularly and the ever-present possibility of having to work out of town, the culture sang to the rigorous tune of corporate stability. But the moment I decided to leave – albeit temporarily – I set the wheels of change in motion and opened the crack for uncertainty. When I finally returned, two years later, I was faced with a number of options: I could return to a professional world I knew with a company that knew me; I could do that same type of work with a different company if I wanted a change in organisational culture; or I could choose something entirely different, within reason.

By this time, I had three years of work experience under the belt and a whole lot more wisdom about the workings of the world. I was far more 'marketable' and knew that, with some perseverance, I could mould my skills and talents in any one of a number of ways when it came to choosing a job. But I was also aware of a need to get settled into something that I could grow with and become really good at. I felt that I had been gallivanting around for long enough, and didn't relish the thought of having to start all over again in a few years' time. For the first time, I started to really feel the tug of the future and the pressure to plot things out according to how they could evolve in time.

Multiple choice

So the career that had seemed so logical a few years ago was now thrown into a mixed bag of possibilities and choices, with no clear path through them all. As far as my consulting option was concerned, I struggled with the issue of lifestyle – a notorious one in management consulting – and the question of my life's passion. While I had, at some point, believed that psychology was the right field for me, I remained underqualified as a psychologist. To become one would mean years more of study, and is that what I really wanted? It wasn't the return to academic life that I was hesitant about, but rather the outcome – did I really aim to be a fully fledged, practising, listen-to-other-people's-problems-all-day psychologist? Or had it just been the semi-interested ramblings of a searching student that had led me to such a degree in the first place? I now had some good experience in business, but I had a long way to go before I really understood all the nuts and bolts – and business is a many and varied thing. So it seems I was underqualified there, too.

Suddenly, my multiple interests and abilities, which had always been such an advantage during the glory days of my schoolgirl past, were becoming a bind. I felt that I had to choose which ones to pursue and which to let fall by the wayside. I am a people's person, so a career like clinical or organisational psychology was an obvious choice. I am a creative person, so I could try branch out into a more artistic realm. I enjoy foreign languages and learn them quickly, so I could try and make a career out of that. I love to sing, so perhaps some intensive lessons and an image makeover could mean a whole new path, too. I am an avid writer in my spare time, so maybe I should look to doing it full-time... . Or maybe I could somehow combine all of these into a jumbled mélange where I could do bits of everything and not have to make a choice! Aaah, if only life were that simple.

At the base of all of this, I felt a familiar sense of internal competition and its accompanying sense of fearful 'what if?'. I kept thinking, 'If I don't make inroads into my career right away, I will be left behind in the race for success. If I choose to do something entirely new, then everyone else will be so far ahead of me and I'll always be playing catch up!' It's an inevitable fact of human nature that we compare ourselves with others; we are social beings, so we naturally tend to judge ourselves according to society's norms. Some people manage to appoint only themselves as the judge and shun the social mean, but most of us do worry about what others will think of us and our choices. And I suppose that's not necessarily a bad thing either, just as long as it doesn't get us down. For me at this point, though, the thought of not achieving in the manner to which I had become accustomed, of falling even further 'behind' my peers than I already was, of not finding my destined career and shining at it... was

enough to really make me panic. What made it even worse was that I didn't feel a strong pull in any particular direction. All options seemed to have equal merit, although some were clearly easier to achieve than others.

Being female added another dimension to my career crisis that I had never really worried about before. You always hears about the classic struggle that a working woman tackles between the opposing forces of her professional and family life. To me, that was a concern for another time and place; I certainly wasn't ready to have children yet and even the thought of being a parent at this stage was enough to make me consult my doctor for extra contraception methods. But yet the possibility of one day having a family of my own suddenly seemed more real, and it had now become a consideration factor in my career crisis. 'Given that I want to have children one day, shouldn't I be working hard at my career now so that it's established by the children stage? Have I wasted valuable time by going travelling and not building a single profession? Should I go to the effort of starting a whole new career when I'm just going to have to put it on hold in a few years' time? But having a job is really important to me – could I really ever give that up for children?' These were the conflicts that plagued me. Just to complicate matters, my husband, who was also going through a similar career crisis now that we were looking for work again, seemed also to be having a gender-related debate. He wondered if he could afford to branch out into a new career and start at the bottom again now that he was supposed to be 'settling down'? Although society has come a long way in terms of male and female equality, he still felt it was expected of him to be the breadwinner, the working partner, the main man. Say he wanted to go back and study again, would that be acceptable at this stage, especially since he now had a wife? And what about the fact that he was 28 and not yet a successful businessman or a thriving entrepreneur – what did that say about his ability to achieve and provide?

The more we agonised over this, the more I realised how central my work was to my definition of myself. And I think that's largely true for most people. After all, you spend the better part of your life either at work, getting to work or leaving work, so it makes sense that your job features prominently on the list of 'what makes you you'. But I hadn't realised quite how integral my career had become to my sense of self-worth; without knowing where I was going, job-wise, I felt less interesting as a person, less meaningful, almost incomplete. One of the first questions that people would ask us while we were travelling – indeed, one of the first questions most people ask when they meet someone new – is 'What do you do?' And by that, they don't mean '... with your spare time' or '... when the sun comes out'. It's the question that hits at the very heart of your validity as a person: first you indicate who you are ('What's your name?'), giving you an identification tag, and then you categorise yourself by having something to 'do' with your life. Having a job, a pursuit, a life's work makes you interesting to talk to and easier to classify; it gives you a conversation starter and a point of reference; it makes you real. Imagine if your response to that question was 'Well, I do... nothing'. Now there's a showstopper. Your new acquaintance would probably smile uncomfortably and excuse him/herself to get a drink. You wouldn't be worth getting to know, you'd be less valid in the greater scheme of this world where doing = being. So having something to 'do' gives us a sense of purpose, even if that purpose is to lie on a beach in the Bahamas and count the grains of sand.

Psychologists might disagree with this concept of identity, or the influence of your work on how you and others view yourself. Psychologically speaking, your identity, self-esteem and self-worth should not be integrally linked to your professional or work identity: a person is inherently worthy, just by virtue of being human. Yet perhaps that is the psychological state for which we should strive. Because Quarterlife reality, particularly in the case of the career crisis, often means that the work issue is pushed to the forefront of your sense of self since that element of your identity is still in the process of being moulded, and is subject to intense questioning and doubt. Certainly for me, my career choice and the indecision about what I was going to do with my life, were primary to how I viewed and valued myself.

And so the debates raged. On the one hand, I considered myself fortunate to even have these career dilemmas in the first place, but on the other, I felt unnerved by uncertainty and fearful of making the wrong choice. It was tempting to stay in the management consulting field, or at least to do something closely related. Going back to my old firm was a comfortable choice: I knew the people, understood the work, had proven myself there, and knew what I had to do to progress. But just because something is snug and cosy, doesn't mean you should spend the rest of your days warming your feet by its fire. I knew that this crossroad was also a chance to get to know myself better and identify the passions that would drive me – even if they turned out to be management consulting again. But I couldn't simply slip back into old ways just because I was too afraid of the new ones. At the very least, I owed it to myself to explore.

WHY THE CAREER CRISIS?

The career element of the Quarterlife Crisis is, like the crisis itself, unique to modern times. A host of issues have conspired to provide more choice to the modern Quarterlifer than to any generation before us:

The technology boom

First and foremost is the technology boom of the 1990s. The explosion of the virtual and hi-tech worlds turned relative youngsters into overnight success stories. Quarterlifers, who shared their coming of age with computers, found themselves in previously unaccustomed territory in which they became the information powerhouses, bearers of a technical ability that their parents' generation simply did not have. As the technology bubble grew, more and more jumped onto the bandwagon, with some finding treasures in binary and hidden millions in code. The world came to accept, if not expect, that tremendous business success is common by the tender young age of 27 and Quarterlifers themselves set their sights on ever-lowering benchmarks for the age at which they should expect career achievement. Of course every bubble must burst, and as technology lost its glow, tons of hopes, dreams and money went down the tubes. But still, Quarterlifers hung on to the possibility of extreme success; a potential had been realised and had set a precedent that was hard to forget. Despite the fact that it was a very small minority who became millionaires in the technology boom and despite the clear evidence of peers who fell with the burst of the tech bubble, Quarterlifers on the whole remained convinced that they should be ready to retire by 35, 40 at the latest. In the aftermath of the boom, many Quarterlifers were left with an unrealistic expectation of the type of success that used to come only with a lifetime of work. What our fathers had achieved by Midlife, we hoped to achieve by Quarterlife. No wonder we beat ourselves up when, at 25, we are still grappling with all the choices out there.

But it's not only in the unrealistic expectations it created that the technology boom helped spearhead the Quarterlife Crisis. Countless Quarterlifers and pre-Quarterlifers, who would hardly have considered technology as a career option, slipped into its wake and obtained diplomas, degrees and jobs in this new-fangled field. In previously unchartered territory, youth and technological potential became desirable qualities in new employees, and job seekers' heads turned towards the hi-tech dream where before they might have sought something else entirely. In my own circle of friends, I have noted numerous examples of how technology lured Quarterlifers previously destined for other fields. Off the top of my head, I can think of seven Quarterlifer friends who now work in the world of computers, Internet and hi-tech, yet only three of them studied information systems at tertiary level. Amongst the others, one, enamoured with saving the earth, got a degree in environmental studies and landed up in a financial services dotcom; one, passionate about industrial design, got a job in technology consulting; one, born for construction and building, headed ultimately for the online world. Only one of these people has been happy in this revised career. The others are reaching the end of their tethers, feeling dissatisfied with technology and facing career crises as they consider other options. They dream of eventually going back to their original calling, realising that technology threw a decoy and led them astray.

You cannot deny that the advent of the technology boom brought with it innumerable opportunities and the promise of a new world. Yet for many, particularly Quarterlifers, it was mere fool's gold, building inaccessible expectations and intensifying the modern career crisis.

Early retirement

Both as a by-product of the technology boom, and as a result of a rapidly changing world, early success in your professional life has become a very real possibility. In the old world of bricks-and-mortar industries, career advancement and promotion were achieved by a steady and often slow rise through the ranks. These days, with an emphasis on youth and adaptability, young people (25–35) are often to be found in senior positions, and since Quarterlifers have embraced the new technology, they are more able than ever to reap extreme success. If I think of the corporate environments in which I worked, early success is a norm. In many of the bigger organisations, the very structure and protocol of the firm make room for career development on merit, regardless of positions filled. In fact, I know of companies where it is possible to achieve the most senior position of 'partner' or 'director' in 12 years. This means that if a reasonably talented graduate joins the firm – say at 23 or 24 years old – he or she could be a senior manager by the age of 30 and even a director by 35; by age 40, that person is ready to retire, having made enough money and gained enough valuable experience to rest happily on his or her laurels.

What is it about our contemporary world that has caused such a redefinition of professional success? Of course the technology boom is the first place winner. Along with this revolution, technology became regarded as the territory of the youth or youthful. I can't even count the number of times I've heard my parents and my friends' parents say things like 'I can never understand how these computers work' or 'I have to wait for my son to come home to show me how to use this e-mail thing'. For the Quarterlife generation and those to follow them, 'these machines' have become a way of life. We can hardly remember typing without Autocorrect or doing correspondence via snail mail. In looking for a job these days, computer skills and technology know-how are advantages, if not prerequisites, so the technology revolution has given the youth a whole new capability platform which our parents' generation simply did not have. Added to this is the exponential rate of change of the modern world. If the world is five times different from how it was only ten years ago, then it must be 50 times different from how it was only 20 years ago, with the technology revolution outstripping even the industrial revolution in terms of reform and change. In such a rapidly altering environment, younger people are generally more adept at anticipating, understanding and exploiting the changes. By their very nature as 'youthful', Quarterlifers have become well positioned to harness transformation and may find themselves in positions of power or seniority far earlier than generations before them.

In this context, it is hardly surprising the Quarterlifers hold an expectation of early success and nurse dreams of retiring at 40 to take up life in a hammock. With such a possibility in mind, the career crisis becomes even more pressing, since 'If I am to retire by 40, I'd better get cracking during Quarterlife. If I don't work hard during my twenties and thirties, I'll never achieve that early target'. As such, Quarterlifers feel compelled to get the ball rolling as soon as possible, causing conflict with other possible pursuits such as travelling the world as a backpacker, or spending time finding the right career. Of course, the problem with all of this is that when 25-year-olds see that their Quarterlife peers have been very successful, and that 45 is not too early to own that luxury yacht, they are only evaluating a small percentage of the working population. They don't see the other vast majority who haven't been over-whelmingly successful, or who slumped when the technology bubble burst, or who gave it all up to do a computer course only to find that there was a glut of computer literates on the market and they would have been better off sticking with their sociology major. Newspapers and talk shows attach no hype or glamour to those stories and Quarterlifers persist with the myth that accelerated success – and early retirement – is typical.

Financial realities

Yet despite the lure of early success and the supposed potential for early retire-ment, actualities of the modern world point gravely to the difficult financial situation which most Quarterlifers face. Studies at London's King College[1] indicate that the modern Quarterlifer generation, particularly those under 30 with middle-class back-grounds, can expect a lower standard of living than that of their parents. Job insecurity, higher taxes, longer working hours, rising property prices, student loans – these are factors which prey on the financial gain which Quarterlifers can anticipate, increasing the pressure on them to pursue the right job and earn the right kind of money, and exacerbating stress levels. Research in Britain shows that between 1993 and 2000, the proportion of people under 25 who owned their own property declined from 21 per cent to 19 per cent and continues to fall. The number of 25- to 29-year-old men living with their parents increased from 18 per cent to 23 per cent between 1978 and 1998. Yet Quarterlifers are reluctant to talk about the financial problems they face, the struggles of paying off student loans, or not being able to afford a home or a family as their parents could when they were their age. Money becomes a crucial driver in the search for a career and may supersede some of the softer issues related to job satisfaction. What's more is that Quarterlifers fear that having a degree today is simply not enough to find the right kind of job since there are so many eligible candidates out there and financial pressures don't allow you to simply settle for any position that is available. Britain's BBC[2] reports that, amongst today's graduates, the average amount owed is a whopping £11,000 – no wonder so many Quarterlifers feel that they've got to get out there and start earning... fast!

So the career crisis of Quarterlife hinges not only on the availability of too much choice and lofty expectations, but also on the harsh (although perhaps unspoken) reality that most of us will have to work harder and longer to gain a financial status that, in real terms, is worth less and is more insecure than ever before.

Equality

Through the ages leading up to our current day, epic struggles have been fought in the name of equality. Equal opportunity for all, regardless of gender, race, age and physical capability, has been the rallying cry as our forefathers and foremothers paved the way for a new world. The professional environment has been a key battleground in this struggle and it wasn't so long ago, in many places around the world, that women doing the same jobs as men were paid considerably less, or that people of colour were denied entry into academic institutions. As the years wore on, many countries and organisations revised their separatist ways so that today, those fortunate enough to enjoy democracy are protected by constitutional and human rights which proclaim equality of treatment.

Of course, with freedom comes choice, and with choice comes confusion. For example, as a middle- or upper-class woman in the West 50 years ago, your generally accepted task (certainly since the Victorian era) was to bear your children and run your home. It was unlikely that you would experience the conflict between career and family because the option of career didn't exist for many women. (This changed during World War II when women began entering the workforce in mass quantities.) However you might have felt about this gender imbalance, your life's path was almost certainly clearer and more defined than that of the modern woman.

Today, as a woman, you should have equal career choices and the right to be rewarded based on merit rather than gender. While this is obviously a triumph, and while not to diminish the struggle for equality, it is also true that the extra dimension of a skilled career adds another level of complexity and stress to the modern woman's life. This is particularly relevant since the societal expectation of women raising the children and managing the home has not diminished at the same rate of dissolution as gender inequality.

So while equality in the workplace has brought about professional validity and helped to further define 'freedom', it has also augmented the host of opportunities which face modern Quarterlifers, intensifying the multiple factors which can characterise the career crisis.

New-age job seeking

With the revolution of our modern world and the dawn of the information era, the job-hunting and recruitment environment has undergone considerable changes, too. This is no longer the world of 35-year-long employment histories or hand-written application forms. The very nature of jobs and the manner in which we find them have been altogether transformed.

Job hopping. Potential employers no longer frown upon job hopping, provided it is limited and particularly during the first few years of an individual's career. The working world has come to understand that a myriad options exist for job seekers and that these days people – particularly in the Quarterlife generation – may have more than one career consideration. Whereas in the past, recruiters would consider anything less than five years at one company to be a show of disloyalty or unreliability, contemporary employers realise that recruits may well test the waters and find their feet before committing wholeheartedly to their employment of choice. Of course this means that Quarterlifers, aware that it is professionally acceptable to consider other viable opportunities, may feel less bonded to a single job – especially if it is their first. Yet, while the option to explore may be attractive, it may also initiate anxiety inherent in the realisation that your path is actually a maze.

Job hunting. There are many ways to skin a cat. Remember the days of searching the weekly classifieds to find the job postings? And remember when you had to mail your typewritten Curriculum Vitae to the human resources manager and wait weeks for a response? Not anymore! Job hunting has taken on an entirely different form. To find a job you can still wade through the classifieds, but you can also search the Internet and go directly to a company's website to find out what's available, or log on to a recruitment site to search according to job type, salary, location, Friday dress code, or proximity to a dry cleaner. You have an interview with recruitment agents who will then match your skills and preferences to job opportunities on their books, or you can check out local universities' graduate recruitment programmes to see who's offering what. Having found your employment selection, you can then e-mail your CV directly to the recruiter concerned, adding as many virtual bells and whistles as you think may increase your chances, or you can post your CV on the many recruitment websites so that employers come to you. Of course, if all else fails, you can still always call up your contacts from your dad's school days or your co-star in last year's community theatre production and beg for an introduction to their company – some old methods never die!

The point is that it's easy to become bombarded by the multiplicity of job-finding methods available and it's even easier to become despondent when the 500 online recruitment sites you visited yield sweet nothing. The sheer number of possibilities, both in terms of possible jobs and in terms of possible ways of securing them, is vast and it's not surprising that today's job seekers may feel overwhelmed.

Booming business. Not only are there more ways to skin the job-cat these days, but there are simply more jobs. Bull or bear markets notwithstanding, the actual variety in the types of businesses in the modern world has increased dramatically from the bricks-and-mortar days. The technology boom has undoubtedly had a lot to do with that, opening up whole spheres for computer wizards, Internet fundis, software developers and so on, with the web of associated industries. The title 'hi-tech crime detective' didn't even exist a few years ago! This is not to say that finding a job is necessarily easy, but rather that the degree of choice is great since business interests and industries have burgeoned.

Information junkies. With the rise of technology and a rapidly changing world, knowledge has become a widespread commodity. Where previously, information was the preserve of the elite, modern technology and the Internet have levelled the playing field, providing open access to content and knowledge. So not only do Quarterlifers muddle along in a world of possibility, they are fully aware of and able to research the options that exist. The information age has brought along with it the picks and shovels to sift through the bulk, so that Quarterlifers are more aware of jobs and job availability than previous generations. And if you've read this far, you'll be familiar with the leitmotif of the Quarterlife Crisis: many options = more indecision = possible crisis.

The war for talent. Modern-day organisations are all too familiar with the concept of the 'war for talent' – the growing contest amongst companies to attract and retain the right types of employees. Young and desirable job seekers – the Quarterlifers – are particularly well equipped to adapt to change and suit multiple business environments. So the war for talent has meant that employers look further afield to find the right candidates, not necessarily limiting themselves to those with the 'correct' degrees or directly applicable qualifications. Once again, this means an increase in job options for Quarterlifers. On leaving university or entering the working world, Quarterlifers begin to discover that their Bachelor of Arts degree does not necessarily come with the limits they had anticipated, or that their year abroad has not counted against them in the race for employment. As thinking, new-age individuals, with the ability to learn and embrace change, employers realise their potential as skilled and contributing members of the workforce, particularly considering the sophistication of the training programmes that many companies offer. So the network of prospects swells even further, and adds fuel to an already blazing fire.

New-age jobs. The career crisis: modern, unique, and often integral to Quarterlife. I can't tell you how many Quarterlifers I have encountered who zero in on the career aspect as primary. And it's not only the educated who experience this crisis, although having an education does broaden your possibilities in life and therefore heightens the feeling of being overwhelmed by choice. School-leavers, and those who do not study beyond secondary level, are also aware of the multitude of possibilities that the modern world offers. Certainly, the new age has also brought with it the freedom to 'be what you want to be', and that often extends beyond the boundaries of the more traditional professions. Never before have we been able to break limits, make new rules, and go beyond the confines of convention to such an extent. These days, it is not uncommon to carry a wallet full of business cards bearing such never-before-seen titles as Lifestyle Practitioner, Body Alignment Therapist, Feng Shui Coordinator, or Pilates Instructor. The new age has also brought with it a renewed interest in health, lifestyle, and alternative living, creating realms of opportunity where little existed before. Individuals are more prepared than ever to go out on a limb in order to find their niche. And, of course, this has meant yet another distinct increase in the possibilities open to the job seeker, creating an open playground for the Quarterlife Crisis.

* * * * * *

It is an ancient Chinese curse to 'live in interesting times'. And since our times are nothing if not interesting, it's hardly surprising that many Quarterlifers feel the burden that comes with the benefits of a brave new world. As the world turned, so too did our expectations of what it means to be eligible for a certain field, or achieve success, or pursue a passion. The career crisis of Quarterlife strikes when one should rather be bathing in the immortal and invincible horizons of young adult life. Instead, the world becomes more real, and more boundless than ever before – a pretty picture with no frame. Just opening my eyes and looking around me at friends, colleagues, and Quarterlifer peers, I began to see the telltale signs of a crisis I thought was my very own sleeping dragon. The Quarterlifers I observed, while all with very different stories unique to the individual, battled the same fundamental question of 'what should I do?' – be it at the start of their career search or even some way through it during the Quarterlife years. Like Michael, for example, who couldn't decide what subjects to take at university so 'I chose to try a variety of courses. But then I graduated and suddenly I had no idea what I was going to do with it all. I thought I'd know by now what I wanted to do after college. But things aren't any clearer, despite all the areas I've tried out'. Or there's Marion – a qualified doctor studying to become a specialist, following a career that she's always wanted to pursue. But just months before she qualified, she started questioning this choice. 'I'm 30 years old and I've realised that the world is bigger than my operating theatre,' she said. 'I'm skilled, I'm adaptable, and I could do more than what I'm trained to do. Maybe I should take a chance and try something new.'

As full-time operatives in the new age, many Quarterlifers can't help but parry with the career-crisis demon as they face an ever-widening scale of opportunity.

SOLUTIONS AND SUGGESTIONS

So what to do about what you do? Aha, now there's the million-dollar question! I certainly don't profess to know all the answers and nothing I suggest is set in stone, by any means. But I can tell you what's worked for me and give you some ideas that may be of value.

When I returned from my honeymoon and started delving into the Quarterlife Crisis, I tackled my career crisis first. I had already had the niggling thought that management consulting was possibly not my final road, so I started looking at the things that other people had said about my talents and compared them with the elements of my jobs that I had really enjoyed. I came up with one clear-cut parameter: creativity. I knew that my shirt-and-collar corporate world, while immensely gratifying in many ways, lacked that innately creative flair that I loved. I had pandered to that element of myself outside work: I took singing lessons, painted ceramics, played the piano, and enjoyed creative writing. But I had never thought of those things in terms of a career – they were hobbies, not jobs. Now, as I re-evaluated and allowed myself to consider other options, I realised that it was mostly possible to turn those sideline interests into mainstream pursuits, and I began to weave new prospects.

The next chapter, which deals with the crisis around passions and dreams, describes how I came to identify my own passion for creative writing and the path that led me to writing this book. From the career-crisis perspective, however, this was a long-awaited journey that forced me to consider a profession as a writer. It wasn't a huge leap of faith. I had majored in English at university and romanticised magazine journalism or a career in creative writing, but I hadn't had the impetus or the guts to pursue it thus far. Now, I was at a crossroads with my career. I had subverted, to some degree, those risk-aversive and fearful elements of my personality by taking the plunge in my move to London and my travels; and I had a unique chance to seek out something innovative and different as far as jobs were concerned. Suddenly, the pull towards writing was stronger than any other, and I owed it to myself to try. After discussing this revelation with my manager at my old consulting firm, I decided to officially resign and commit wholeheartedly to this new career attempt. As my manager said, 'Consulting will always be there; this chance may not. You're young and able, with an incredibly supportive husband and relatively few commitments. If you're going to jump, jump now.'

So I did. I set myself some targets, drew out a timeline and went about the flurry of understanding a whole new industry. It's funny how, once you stick your nose in an area that you're really passionate about, opportunities seem to come knocking. Before I knew it, I was three chapters into this book, eight magazine articles down the line, and in discussions for some exciting new projects. At the same time, I looked at doing some freelance management consulting with an associate, just to keep my mind partly attuned to an area I still enjoyed. And I signed up for volunteer work since my time was now flexible and I wanted to be 'useful' in as many ways as I possibly could be. Most of all, I stopped worrying so much. The world has enough Internet businesspeople, lawyers and accountants without me clogging up the works. If I ever decided that I wanted to be back in management consulting or that psychology was really my true love, then I'd face that decision when I got to it. I started to see the present as critical since the future is a damn hard nut to crack. At that point, the option of launching a writing career was more possible than whimsical because I was in the driving seat and prepared to face the challenge. If it flopped, then at least I'd have tried – regret is an awful bedtime companion. I gave myself a time limit during which to determine whether a career in writing was really for me, but once I'd set that ultimatum, I put it aside and tried to focus entirely on the task at hand; I would re-evaluate at the end of that time limit, and only then. For now, it was me, my laptop and the long, hard slog to the publishing grail.

There are a few fundamental issues that I think helped in my decision to change careers and relax about the future. There are also some other general truths or techniques described below that may be worth a try if you find yourself facing a career crisis.

Reality check 1: Great expectations

Newsflash: it's not normal to have 3 BMWs and a secretary by the age of 24. It takes a while to achieve success and most people work a lifetime for it. The problem is that twenty-somethings see others who have been very successful at a relatively young age and wonder how they compare; but they only see the one per cent who may have achieved that success – they don't see the other 99 per cent who have not, since the story of the majority isn't what makes news headlines or conversation at cocktail parties. It's important to be realistic about what you can achieve, and by when. That's not to say that you shouldn't dream or have ambitions, but rather that you should frame those aspirations in a realistic context and not set yourself up to fail just because you misjudged the norm. Particularly insofar as the technology boom is concerned, understand that it's not all dollar signs and glamour – certainly not since the burst of the dot-com bubble – and that you should never underestimate the value of hard work and sound business. Once, very briefly, it was possible to run a company held together by bubble gum and matchsticks. Yet, as nature would have it, the world corrected itself and once again, the professional world turned to the irrefutable reliability of fundamental business principles which had often been ignored or transgressed in the Internet explosion. Business got back to the business of doing good business. So if you've got a choice, go for salt-of-the-earth rather than fly-by-night, and let a healthy combination of sense and passion rule when choosing your career.

Reality check 2: Knowledge isn't what it used to be

Where knowledge was previously the preserve of the elite, it has now become the staple diet of all. The Internet has made information wholly accessible to anyone, rendering useless the old equation that knowledge = power. The repercussions of this information explosion are numerous:

- It means that you can't turn up at a job interview with no understanding of what the business or the position is about. Enough information is available out there – through the Internet, libraries, careers offices to really build your knowledge and wow your prospective employers with how much you already know about them. And that also goes for the information that you may require to make a decision about which career to choose or which job to apply for. Research your options well and make sure that, if nothing else, you are clued-up about the choices you have and what they may involve. There's no excuse not to know. Acquire knowledge as a baseline for judgement, and let the decisions you make be informed ones.

- It means that the rest of the world can access much of the same information that you can, so there are new challenges for staying ahead of your game. Innovation and skill become critical in setting yourself apart.

- It means that since knowledge is no longer the rarity it once was, the ability to manipulate knowledge has become vital, gaining the savvy to use information to your advantage. One of the key ways to acquire this ability is through experience: exposure to your chosen area of interest and interaction with relevant individuals is part of the recipe for success. And sometimes, there's just no substitute for time in the saddle.

Reality check 3: You are not old

Realise that, as a Quarterlifer, you are not old! The issue of age is a chapter in itself, but as far as career goes, it's important to understand that Quarterlife is your once-in-a-lifetime chance to discover what you, as an adult, are all about. Rushing into a career that will bore you to tears or cause endless sighs of complaint and dissatisfaction, is hardly the way to optimise that chance. Even if you only find your career destiny at age 35, you've still got a good 30 years of work left in you to make a success of it. It's hardly a tragedy if you spend a couple of years before that trying other things or seeing the world. Take advantage of your early Quarterlife years. When you're younger, you learn more easily, are quicker to synthesise information, and are far more adaptable to change, so Quarterlife is a genetically appropriate time to experiment with your career. If you aren't one of those people who has known their whole life what they want to be when they grow up, then consider Quarterlife your crash course in discovering your answers. If you are one of those people who looks around after two years in a job and realises that there's no way you can do this for the rest of your working life… move on and take a chance with something that may well turn out to be your professional destiny. And try not to fall into the trap of feeling trapped. Realise that, being young, you are malleable, and if you found a job or started a business or got a degree once, chances are you could do it again.

Reality check 4: Every job has a bad hair day; manage your own career

Even if you do find your ideal job, or manage to follow your dreams, chances are you'll still have down days. Even the so-called perfect job has faulty times when you wish you were anywhere but there, doing anything but that. So don't give up or job just because it hits a few flat spots now and then − it doesn't mean it's not the right one, it just means that you're as human as the rest of us. Be careful not to be too hasty in your judgement of your job or career. If you are experiencing problems or too many down days at work, consider whether the issues are circumstantial (and hence transient and solvable) or indicative of deeper, more serious concerns which may require a complete re-evaluation of your situation. Even if you work for someone else, you are still responsible for managing your own career and making sure that you derive the maximum benefit and fulfilment. You may well have a boss, but no-one's going to look after you like you look after yourself. So work at your job, wring the optimal potential from it, and forgive it its occasional dull moments.

Open your eyes and ears

While ignorance may be bliss, and may help stave off a career crisis for a time, it is certainly not the most enriching way to live. Try not to insulate yourself. Explore your career options and don't be afraid to know what's out there. The world tolerates a degree of job hopping or career uncertainty because it understands the unique challenges that modern Quarterlifers face. As part of that unique generation with many choices at your fingertips, you deserve to avail yourself of information and opportunities. While the thought of too many options, or the possibility of leaving a comfort zone behind is often scary, job dissatisfaction and regret are even scarier.

Use your resources

With the information age at our beck and call, knowledge is far easier to come by. So if and when the career crisis hits, call up the resources available to help identify the professions that may interest you or to understand the job market. Use the Internet to search for information, to encounter different companies and industries, to broaden your market knowledge, to understand what jobs are available, and even to make an application. If you are a recent graduate or have access to a university, visit the campus careers office to sign up for company presentations or to read through the job literature. Consider talking to a careers counsellor – they aren't solely for use by scholars or students – and get to know yourself and your abilities. If you have a particular job interest but aren't sure about what it's like in real life, inquire about shadowing someone in a similar position or visiting a relevant company to chat with people who have experience in that area. Build up a voracious appetite for information. Know that your decision is likely to be greatly facilitated if you really understand the pros, cons and realities of a certain job. We haven't been part of a knowledge revolution for nothing – take advantage of it!

Talk and listen

There are few things in life as valuable as experience. As far as resources go, other people's experience is one of the most helpful you will find. Learn to talk and to listen. If you are juggling career options, or feeling directionless, or struggling to identify your niche, tell someone. There's a fair chance that they will be going through much the same thing or will have some nugget of advice that can help. Build your allies and your network of contacts so that you have a source from which to draw solace, inspiration and ideas. Don't be afraid to ask someone about their job if you find it interesting. Use your contacts – they may just yield what you are looking for.

Diagnose 'multiple personality advantage'

You may be good at more than one thing as far as careers go. Just because your 10th Grade aptitude test showed that you'd make a good journalist doesn't necessarily mean that you wouldn't also be a great concert pianist. And although having multiple skills may increase your possibilities and make the career decision harder, it also raises your chances of identifying a profession that you can be passionate about and allows you to draw on various talents to inspire your work. I met one Quarterlifer, Rael, who studied architecture, worked in the technology world after graduation, took a year off to travel, returned home to pursue an interest in photography as a scout for a film company, and now works in property development. He says, 'I went from knowing, without even thinking, that I would be an architect, to juggling so many career possibilities that I could hardly count them all. At one stage I felt really torn, but I eventually saw that my multiple talents were a talent in themselves. After agonising about choosing a single career, I thought about all the jobs I've held, and realised that I've built a web of valuable skills. I may just be one of those people who are great at ten things rather than brilliant at one. So, until I find the area of interest that overrides all others, I should stop stressing about it and use my various talents to my advantage rather than trying to cram myself into a single profession. None of the experience I gain is a waste.'

Try not to get railroaded into a career simply because of a single proficiency. Consider your interests and your abilities and try to find the middle ground between skill and passion.

The road to riches is paved with passion

I remember when I took all those aptitude and intelligence tests at school. The counsellor told me that I must not take Science as a final-year subject because my aptitude for History was much higher; if I took Science, I wouldn't score higher than a C or a D. As it happened, I was far more interested in Science than I was in History and, being unsure of what career I wanted to choose after school, I thought that Science would probably be more useful in the long run. So, against all advice, I took Science for my matriculation year. And I got an A. I enjoyed the subject infinitely more than I would have enjoyed History and undoubtedly excelled at it because my interest increased my willingness to work hard. So it seems to be true that passion is a key to success. If you love your work, you are bound to achieve at it (while the opposite is also true).

Too often, particularly as modern Quarterlifers, we are attracted to a profession by the false promise of glamour and success rather than our innate ability and interest in that area. I need only think of one friend who, like so many others, chased the technology dream over and above his passion for art and design. After four fruitless years in the IT business, having held three different but unfulfilling jobs, he was finally made redundant and decided to return to the art world where he is now infinitely happier. 'I had to be forcibly turned out of a job to see that I shouldn't even have been there in the first place,' he said recently. Of course, it's not always so easy to just give it all up for the sake of passion. Financial concerns are primary and often govern the choice of career, particularly for Quarterlifers who are just starting out. But I must quote my locally famous hairdresser who always says: 'If you are passionate about what you're doing, you will always have money in your pocket!' I want to believe that he's right. You may not be rolling in dough, but at least you'll have motivation, fulfilment and drive on your side – and with those ingredients, financial rewards are almost certain.

Throw caution to the wind

Before I left for London and my subsequent travels, I was as cautious as a tightrope walker, carefully plotting my next steps and always setting up a safety net to catch me if I fell. But the decision to leave my comfortable job behind and abandon all for a temporary life change, while still 'safe' in some respects because of my leave of absence, did help nudge my circuits and set the caution switch at least to standby. Then I returned home and found that, not only was everything still standing, but my options were broader and more exciting than ever before. I came to understand that healthy risks are often worth taking and that although it might be easier to spend your life in a comfort zone, it's not always the best or most fulfilling choice. As a

Quarterlifer, you have the advantage of youth and 'bouncebackability' on your side. It's a special time in your life when risks, particularly career-oriented ones, can be well hedged against the security of knowing that you've still got your whole life ahead of you to get it right. For Quarterlifers who don't have children, the ability to take a chance on a job is even greater, since your primary responsibility and accountability is to yourself. Of course, there is a difference between taking a risk and being irrational. Some job options or business ideas are sounder than others and if you are hoping to make millions selling ice to Eskimos, you are likely to be sorely disappointed. It's always wise to be wise, but at the Quarterlife stage, you have more leeway for mistakes. So rather than bemoaning your fate for having too many choices or not enough direction, throw caution to the wind and get out there – you never know what you might find.

Don't dare to compare

Resist the temptation to compare yourself with your peers. Firstly, because unless you are particularly close to a person, you never really know what's going over in someone else's life. While things may appear calm and focused from the outside, that's not always the case. Secondly, comparison is dangerous when you're dealing with apples and oranges rather than apples and apples. People are unique, which means their life circumstances differ from each other's and comparison is inevitably invalid. What is important to one person is not necessarily important to the next. It is very common for Quarterlifers – particularly those who are weighing up the options of travelling vs studying further vs pursuing a career – to fear being left behind by their peers. I know that when I was considering leaving my consulting job for a year, it was difficult to think that the colleagues who had joined the firm at the same time as I had would gain a year's advantage over me in terms of promotion, pay and experience. Having taken the plunge, though, I now realise that those fears were unnecessary – primarily since I have landed up in an entirely different career anyway. But even if I had returned to work at my old job, and all my old colleagues were so much more advanced that I was, what difference would it really have made in the grander scheme of things? I gained experience of an entirely different and invaluable kind. Nor did my friends, family or colleagues 'look down' on me at all for having taken the time 'off'. Instead, they envied my experiences and my superiors valued the added insight and flavour those experiences would have brought to my work.

So what if you are a few years 'behind' your school classmate in terms of building your career? If you've spent the time figuring out what you really want to do, or gaining valuable life experience that will be difficult to recapture later, it becomes insignificant that John Doe has two more years of experience in a single job. With a potential 40 years in the working world, a couple of years of scouting around at the start are hardly worth stressing about. Rather find the right job five years after the person next to you, than have to change careers 15 years down the line because your heart can't handle the pressure of discontent and disappointment. Try to consider the bigger picture to understand whether the comparison you are drawing between yourself and another is really suitable or necessary.

Become interesting again

Remember when you were 12 years old and you spent most of your afternoons schlepping from one extra mural activity to another? In all likelihood, now that you're an adult, you don't have time to play soccer, or go for guitar lessons, or join a dance class; you're busy working during the day and exhausted by the time the evening or the weekend rolls around. The truth is that, just because you're an adult, doesn't mean you have to give up on the interests which diversified your skills, massaged your additional talents, and made you a far more interesting, multidimensional person. Of course, as you enter and progress in the working world, it becomes difficult to manage your time and save your energy for activities outside work. But just because it's more challenging, doesn't mean it should be impossible. Remain conscious of the things you enjoy, in addition to your work, and try not to lose out on the value that they can add. Certainly, it takes a lot more effort, but try and build your hobbies into your life, even if it means that you get home to your couch an hour or two later; chances are, you will have released some stress and will come home a happier person.

Getting involved in hobbies can also broaden your social circle to include people with similar interests, helping to ease that other Quarterlife blow that comes with friends moving on or your own realisation that your school mates just don't know you so well anymore. I know that my hobbies have become a vital method of dealing with some of my Quarterlife-Crisis anxiety. During my first year of work after graduation, I let all my interests slide because I was so focused on settling into my job – which I think is fair since a new job is a lot to deal with. But by the time the second year came around, I realised that there were parts of me that were missing and my job wasn't enough to take their place. I could hardly develop my love for singing while at the office! So I slowly started introducing my hobbies back into my life and found that, not only did my managers not mind that I left work five minutes early on a Monday to be on time for my singing lesson, but they actually appreciated my endeavour to cultivate a life outside of work. So don't let your hidden talents slide. Who knows, you may even choose to convert one of those hobbies into a full time career one day, saving yourself lots of hassles when you hit Midlife!

Define yourself beyond work

It is tempting to let a career become our be-all and end-all. Considering that work is how we spend the majority of our time, it's not surprising that our job title is often central to our self-definition, particularly during the Quarterlife years when we are in the process of discovering and refining that very feature of our lives. Yet while the willingness to work hard and the desire to pursue a successful and rewarding career is admirable, work is not the sole factor that comprises identity. As human beings, we have multiple functions in life and we should take care to nurture all sides of ourselves. Whether you have chosen dentistry, engineering, child rearing, or scuba diving as your full-time occupation, it is only one part of you; and while you should be able to declare that occupation proudly since it is likely the biggest part of you, remember that there is more to you than that one label. You may consider your other facets secondary, but they are also central to your personality and, if celebrated, can add significantly to your own concept of yourself. If neglected, they can leave you feeling unfulfilled and lopsided. So strive for a sense of balance in your life, for appropriate proportions of work, play, family, friends and self. Yes, Quarterlife is the time when you are primed to establish your career, and have the energy to build it vigorously, but that should not necessarily exclude other elements of your life which may be important to you and also require nurturing. Achieving balance is something that many people struggle for many years to do; if you feel that it is a worthwhile concept, you may as well get started on it early!

Face the fear of failure

Every one of us has to face failure at some point, whether it's losing a running race, flunking an exam, or feeling like you've disappointed someone important to you. For some, failure is just a necessary inconvenience en route to success, so picking yourself up and starting again – stronger and wiser – is the constructive attitude. For others, failure is a punishment worse than death and the fear of failure can become immobilising. I think I generally fall into the latter category, particularly regarding the idea of failing publicly. I remember not telling anyone when I went to take my driver's licence test, in case I didn't pass; that way, no-one would be any the wiser and I could simply keep trying until I succeeded. Even today, with writing this book, I get a tiny clutch of fear every time I even talk about it because, despite how much I may believe in the project, I am terrified that it will fail. Of course, having the support and excitement of people around me is a blessing, but it also means that they will be watching to see if it all comes tumbling down. But then I think about the potential benefits of quelling my fear and pursuing this dream, and I honestly don't have a choice but to forge ahead, despite the potential embarrassment of finding that my husband was the one who bought all the unsold books.

The Quarterlife Crisis is primetime for the fear of failure, particularly regarding the career crisis. What if I'm not good at my job? What if I fall behind my peers? What if I leave this job and have to start again at the bottom somewhere? What if I choose the wrong job and land up being miserable in years to come? On and on the questions stream… all annoying yet scary at the same time, like those awful spinning teacups at a funfair. But the truth is, failure is part of life. Whether it's large (like being the CEO of Enron when your company is in the midst of a fraud scandal) or small (like burning the cake you were baking for your mother-in-law), failure is as normal as breathing. It's the way we learn

The Quarterlife phase of life demands that we tackle the fear of failure head-on, since the decisions we start to make are bigger than ever before and we feel that they may hold more serious repercussions than any we've made up to now. As we face the challenge of Quarterlife, we begin to question the status quo and slowly shed the skin of the past, leaving fears and anxieties freshly exposed. Facing insecurities is one of the most difficult tests to endure. Certainly, it is often difficult to be honest with ourselves and to accept that life is less than perfect, and taking chances raises the odds in failure's favour, so why expose ourselves even further? Yet there's a resounding truth in the old saying 'nothing ventured, nothing gained', particularly insofar as the Quarterlife career crisis is concerned. The determination of your professional destiny is a voyage of discovery, and no-one ever discovered anything with a blindfold round their eyes and cottonwool in their ears. If you fail – so what? If you are young and able, open and honest, interested and ambitious, with just a smidgen of resolve… you'll survive. And not only will you survive, you'll thrive on what you learn in the process. Be open to your options, be frank with yourself about yourself, and open the door when opportunity knocks.

Go with the flow

What do you do if you're up the creek without a paddle? Ain't nothing to do but go with the flow, praying that you'll pick up a branch along the way. You may feel that your career crisis is leaving you at a complete impasse; you may feel that the options are too numerous to even contemplate, or the opportunities too scary to attempt. Or simply that there's nothing out there that's just right for you. You are not alone. You aren't the first and won't be the last to tread these waters. Often, the value of a crisis is in the experience thereof: the tolerance you build and the insight you gain is of far more value than if you'd found a job on day one after graduation. It is certainly no joy ride, and you'll wish more than once that you had brought a helmet, but the knocks are bruises only and you'll get there in the end. Accept that this is a trying time in your life; understand that it's a journey to be endured and a rite of passage which is both your burden and your blessing to bear. The light is out there – go grab it.

1 **Source:** *The Sunday Times* (South Africa), 7 July 2002
2 **Source:** BBC News (online), 8 August 2002

WHAT IS MY PASSION? [the dream crisis]

I devoured ballet books as a child. Afternoons would find me in the library, making a beeline for the stories about Sadlers Wells and the lucky girls who found their dreams *en pointes*. I was a part-time dancer too, diligently spending three afternoons a week prancing around one of the local church halls, steeped in the world of tutus and hair glue. My dream was to become a prima ballerina, of twirling away to the gasp and applause of an appreciative audience as I executed another flawless pirouette. I conveniently ignored my declining ballet exam results and scoffed at my older siblings who came to an eisteddfod and hosed themselves as I lumbered off in one direction while the rest of my group went in another. Their conviction that I would be more suited to play a baby elephant in the 'Lion King' than a fairy in 'Swan Lake' did nothing to dull my ambitions. Then I hit puberty, and a prematurely bulging chest and the untimely appearance of womanly thighs began to wreak havoc on my willingness to wear a leotard and tights. Boys and studies now ranked higher in the hierarchy of extracurricular activities, and my satin slippers slowly collected dust. Dreams started shifting: I imagined being a pop star, crooning away to wild fans. I discovered a flair for languages and pictured myself as a translator at the United Nations, jetting my way through a multilingual existence. I even stuck glow-in-the-dark stars on my ceiling, dreaming of being an astronaut and exploring unnamed planets. I cultivated a rich and vibrant fantasy life. Dreaming was easy.

But something changed as I got older. The closer I got to Quarterlife, and the nearer I got to choosing a dream, the fuzzier the reception on my fantasy box became. Despite the acquisition of knowledge and education, I began to lose touch with those visions. Perhaps they were childish, the stuff of unrealistic imaginings only, but I didn't replace them with anything more concrete or achievable. I just stopped dreaming.

University was a time spent doing haphazard taste tests of some of the options. I dabbled. Rather than immersing myself in any one field, I flitted, birdlike, from one tree to another, hoping to find one in which to make a nest. Some seemed more eligible than others. The idea of law was interesting for a while and the psychology route was definitely appealing, but neither really grabbed me with the force of a life's passion and shouted: 'pick me, pick me'. I decided to take up a year's postgraduate study in psychology and then to move on to management consulting, decisions that felt logical and suitable rather than passionate and focused. Those were enjoyable times, and I undoubtedly benefited from them, but I never felt that contented glow that comes with knowing that you are pursuing your life's ambition. My dreams had escaped me.

As far as career and future prospects were concerned, I was facing a big wide world filled with possibilities, but lacking a single driving force. In spite of many interests and abilities, there was no single, overriding, blinding, forceful vision of where I saw myself and of what I saw myself doing in 30, or ten or even five years' time. I envied people who seemed to 'just know'. Life appeared to slot into place for others: opportunities came around, apparently without much effort, purely by virtue of the fact that they were destined to be doing what they were doing. I wished for a single-minded motivation and struggled to identify it within myself. I disregarded the unrealistic dreams: there was simply no way I could make it as a pop star despite my love of singing; the astronaut dream was shelved as a childhood fantasy; and you could get enough language practice by going to the odd French restaurant rather than being submerged in linguistics. But I drew blanks when I tried to consider what I still wanted to be – my capacity for dreams seemed to have dried up and, besides, it was hardly practical to centre my life on something that might just be a fantasy.

Then off I went to London and beyond. Before we left London on our four-month trip to Asia and the East, Richard and I made a deal: he would take the photographs if I would do the writing. So I kept a detailed journal and sent lots of e-mails and postcards to our willing audience around the world. Most of what the two of us experienced was completely foreign to those who received my correspondence. Certainly, it was entirely new to us, too. How many people do you know who have shared a Trans-Siberian train compartment with a Mongolian horseman? As our friends downloaded messages from astounding places that had managed to build Internet cafes before flushing toilets, they marvelled at the unique and life-changing moments we were privileged to have. I returned from our adventures renewed and invigorated, having experienced something that is difficult to acquire through any-thing other than travel. True to my contract with Richard, I had filled two notebooks with small print and the e-mailed commentary on our exploits wove vivid stories about our forays into some of the world's most weird and wonderful places.

Back on home soil, I was suddenly bombarded by feedback. Independently, people wrote to tell me how much they had enjoyed reading my correspondence, feeling as if they were right there along with us. From friends to work colleagues, from a grandmother to a 12-year-old niece, all of them commented on what they seemed to believe was a talent for writing. Many of them asked why I had not taken writing more seriously before. To my amazement, two people – again independently – had compiled my e-mails into book form, presenting them to me as lasting testimony of an unforgettable trip. And so many offered to forward copies of the e-mails to me, saying that they hadn't been able to bring themselves to delete them just yet. I was gobsmacked! I knew that I had always loved creative writing, but I never thought of it as more than a hobby. Yes, I'd had a couple of articles published, but that was just for fun. Someone reminded me that I had majored in English, but that was for a love of the subject rather than a desire to turn it into a career. Had I hit on something here?

When the umpteenth message flashed in my Inbox, telling me that my e-mails had made a particular friend laugh out loud so many times that she had stopped reading them at work for fear of unfair dismissal, I decided to take the feedback a little more seriously.

'What do you think of all of this?' I asked Richard.

With that smug, know-it-all look that he gets when he knows he's won a bet, he said, 'Did you think it was just to keep you entertained that I always got you to write the introductions and conclusions to my assignments at university, even though you knew nothing about my subjects? Hardly. You've got an ability to weave words on paper, and now others have seen it, too. You know how you always wish you had a passion that drove you or a dream that you could follow blindly? Well, maybe you've just been looking down the wrong rabbit hole to find your niche.'

At that time, I was recuperating at home after an unexpected operation and I knew that it would take a while before I could resume normal life. I was still on a leave of absence from my job, and definitely in no condition to go back to work just yet. My mother was about to produce her second book of social history, which was in need of some editorial review. So I volunteered. For the next few weeks, I immersed myself in a task that felt remarkably rewarding. The written word became my crutch as I slowly built up my stamina and I tried my hand at something that seemed, at the same time, new and second nature to me.

As I crossed t's, dotted i's, and rewrote whole paragraphs, I began to consider the literary field in a far more serious light. Was Richard right? Could I really make a career out of something that seemed so effortless to me as writing? I started thinking about turning a part-time passion into a full-time occupation, but that seemed like too much fun to be considered real 'work'. Yet if I really thought about it, really dug deep, I would have to admit that I probably harboured a sub-conscious fantasy about being a writer. I thought I had forgotten how to dream, yet every time I walked into a bookstore, I would imagine what it would be like to have my own work on the shelves. To be honest, the idea of submitting articles to a magazine or writing a book seemed like dreams I didn't even know I'd had. I now realised that I would actually love to build a career in writing. I just hadn't had the impetus, the guts or even the inspiration to do it so far.

My leave of absence was due to terminate pretty soon, so I knew I had to make a firm decision about what I planned to do. I mulled the idea over in my head until it was pulverised, getting more and more excited about the prospect of a career in writing and building a small hub of ideas about possible projects. The primary one was this book on the crisis that had almost brought my life to a standstill. Imagine putting all my thoughts, findings and observations on paper to share with other people? But I still wondered whether the whole idea was just some fanciful pipe dream rather than an achievable reality.

I decided to have a frank and open discussion with a manager from my old consulting firm, giving her the lowdown on the most recent revelations I'd had and scouring her extremely practical and accomplished brain for the slightest inkling of a thumbs-up. It didn't take much. She immediately supported the idea and made me understand that I could always return to a consulting career, while the writing possibility might not come around again so easily. She believed that this phase of my life was ideal to take such a chance. I didn't have children to support, my husband was behind me one hundred per cent, and so what if I had to beg the neighbours for leftovers until I managed to start generating some meagre income? Of course I was terrified of failure, but Richard insisted that if I didn't try, I'd never know – and that would be the greatest failure of all. As I've said before, regret is a bitter pill to swallow.

The one major concern that I did have was the financial element of this decision, since I couldn't quantify or even necessarily guarantee any income. I still had some savings which I could rely on for a while, but I was reluctant to blow everything I had and further exacerbate financial insecurities. This is where the blessing of marriage and mutual responsibility came to the rescue. Richard insisted that we could manage the early stages of my new career on his salary and that there would be opportunity enough for savings in the future. This took a lot of convincing, I have to say. I didn't relish the concept of being dependent on somebody else for my daily bread – no matter how close I might be to that person and even if he was my husband. I was really fond of being independent and wanted to contribute equally to my marriage and my subsistence. For Richard, this was not an issue. He believed, and convinced me, that this was the only way to go. We could get by; and if it all went bust, well then we'd rather live with 'tried and failed' than 'failed to try'. I convinced myself that, being young and able, I would manage to pick myself up if I crashed. Besides which, if everyone else thought it was such a logical step, then so should I. So I closed my eyes, took a big bite of humble pie, and jumped.

The day after I resigned from my old company, I was tempted to call back and plead temporary insanity induced by too much sun on the beaches of Thailand. I couldn't believe I'd given up a well-paid, socially acceptable job in exchange for some ludicrous attempt to break into an industry I knew nothing about. On top of which, I'd be spending most of my time with only my computer for company. Don't get me wrong, I love a game of Solitaire as much as the next guy, but this was madness!

But a big chunk of humble pie had gotten lodged right in my throat, so there was no way I was admitting defeat just yet. There was nothing to do but get on with it. And that's when I began to understand a truism of this world: if you poke your nose into something new, flying by the seat of your pants with passion as your only fuel, opportunity is bound to arise. Before I had even put finger to keyboard, I found myself sifting through a small molehill of prospects that had come my way. By telling people that I was trying to launch a career in writing, and sending out feelers into this alien territory, I began to track the lay of the land and glean opportunity through contacts, questions and sheer enthusiasm. That's not to say that I was suddenly bombarded by publishers banging on my door promising bloated advances for my work – hardly! But I did see light in this tunnel and felt the throb of promise and opportunity.

I am treating this career change as any job. I plan my hours, establish my targets and have a routine. I'm coming to terms with the fact that this is a start at the bottom of a highly competitive ladder and have given myself a fixed amount of time after which I will evaluate whether or not this is for me. I have investigated doing freelance management consulting so that I can try to keep up with parts of that industry, too. I haven't lost my interest in that area, I have simply decided to follow my heart rather than my head, even if just for this once. That means facing entirely new challenges and experiencing no small measure of self-doubt. Some days are phenomenal – better than I could have imagined – and some days are awful, as with any job, I suppose; but mostly it's good, really good. And if it doesn't work out, well then, it doesn't work out. At least I will have improved my touch-typing. But above all, I keep reminding myself that I am doing this for the love of the game, and that I'm lucky to have found a reachable dream.

WHY THE DREAM CRISIS?

Having a passion or a dream certainly does not guarantee you success in your endeavours, or cancel out the worries and efforts of hard work. It simply means that you have a good chance of enjoying what you do, and that fulfilment becomes a hard currency. As we consider the career choices available, and face the wide-open plains of adulthood, Quarterlifers begin to grapple with the dilemma concerning our life's passion, searching for destiny in a minefield of explosive issues.

The question of career

One of the primary catalysts of the Quarterlife Crisis itself is the question of career. The immense number of opportunities and expectations that Quarterlifers face sets up a possible predicament regarding the choice of job or profession. The dream crisis is often tightly linked to this career crisis, since it revolves around the question of your life's work. Some arrive at Quarterlife intent on a certain career, knowing beyond the shadow of a doubt that they will pursue that particular avenue.

Others arrive at Quarterlife with no inkling of what that path may be, assailed by the multitude of options that materialise. Still others may experience fading dreams, having felt certain, at one stage, that they knew where they were going yet finding later on that they were misguided or had lost interest. Just as the career crisis becomes exacerbated by an increase in prospects, so too does the dream crisis, as Quarterlifers begin to understand that life, and the destiny they seek, may have traced more than one route. Most children believe that they will ultimately become a 'something' – that job or title that will help define them as adults. It's the whole question of 'what will I be when I grow up?'. Now all grown up, Quarterlifers encounter the same issue of job and title, often still not knowing the answer or wondering whether they are on the right road. As the career crisis forms, so too does the dream crisis, extending the question of 'what should I do?' to become one of 'what was I born to do?'.

The technology boom... again

We discussed the technology boom in detail in the previous chapter, and came to understand how its rise created new opportunities and expectations, despite the glint of fool's gold. While the information age yielded newfound passion for some, many others have let slide their childhood ambitions or other-worldly dreams which had nothing at all to do with technology and its by-products. It seems that technology has made it too easy to become engulfed in other people's fantasies, or in the dreams of an age that has seen the most astounding rate of development. It has meant that Quarterlifers, originally bound for other fields, became consumed by the smoke and mirrors of the technology promise. Yet as technology loses its glow with the burst of the dot-com bubble, and as people come to question whether they are destined to be software programmers when they had always wanted to be horticulturalists, the dream crisis becomes apparent and the questions of 'what is my true passion?', and 'what am I destined to be?' assume the forefront. In some ways, technology provided an easy way out for many Quarterlifers. Rather than facing the issue of their work interest or digging deep to find an overriding passion, many walked blindly towards the bright lights and dollar signs of Silicone Valley, and coded their dreams in html. Trying to get a job in London? Try the tech sector. Need a boost to your CV? Do a computer course. Want to impress your girlfriend's parents? Say you've got a job in IT. Technology beckoned, and we ran. It's no wonder so many of us have lost touch with our most innate abilities, our core passions. Certainly, many Quarterlifers feel their dream crises keenly as they lift their heads from computer monitors and find that their original passions have eluded them or that they are too afraid to pursue a faint calling from long ago. They can hit F1 all they like – it's a crisis of dreams for which no Help key has the answer.

Now is the time

Quarterlife is the age of opportunity. It's the time in your life when physical, emotional and mental capacities are at a peak, ready to cope with whatever may come your way. Still glowing with the promise of youth, and yet to be burdened by the concept of your mortality, Quarterlifers become well aware that now is the time to set the wheel's of life in full motion. For many, this becomes a pressing issue of sowing the seeds for financial and social success. Quarterlifers often perceive this stage to be the one where a focus on career should be central, particularly with regard to maximising earning potential and developing status. In many cases, the dreams you had as a youngster or the passions that you thought excited you do not comply with the pressure to earn and advance. For instance, if you had always yearned to travel, and if you now find yourself in a position to do so, you may feel torn between that passion and the need to build your career. Or perhaps you were always enthusiastic about nursing but find that you are disappointed by the salary prospects: your need or desire to make money in these, your most able years, con-flicts with the passion you have for the profession. Perhaps we have come to value material success and prestige over passion. Certainly, the feasibility of success at a relatively young age, and the perceived pressure on Quarterlifers to make their mark as early as possible, has pushed career and financial success to the vanguard of the 20–35ers' assault on adult life. Passion and dreams may become relegated to the sidelines, particularly if they are not perceived as 'sensible' or 'practical'. Yet it's difficult to ignore our core and often, passion niggles at us to show that it still counts in the pursuit of our life's work. When passion and ambition clash, when there is no middle ground between dreams and drive, crisis lurks.

Being normal

As children, and particularly as teenagers, we instinctively compare ourselves with others, weighing our individuality against the norm. Social psychology teaches us that this process of assessment is part of growing up, that by understanding how we compare with our friends or contemporaries, we begin to form our own identities and to comprehend the society in which we live. How well we remember the teenage angst of trying to fit in and negotiating peer pressure; how well we remember the parental disputes over our bid to pierce a fifth earring hole, just because Jenny/Jimmy/James/xxx had got one. As we enter Quarterlife, the habits of comparison die hard, if ever, and most of us look around to see what everyone else is doing before doing something ourselves. Moreover, society holds its own expectations of what we should or shouldn't be pursuing, should or shouldn't be achieving, with the result that we tend to restrict ourselves – career-wise, relationship-wise, lifestyle-wise – to what we regard as socially acceptable. For some, this web of suitability is smaller than for others, governed by social, cultural, religious or political circles. For many, fanciful concepts like dreams or passions become secondary to the 'normal' pursuits that are seen to guarantee success, reward and acceptance.

Yet the Quarterlife stage is also the one at which we begin to carve our own individual niche, blending our unique mix of talents and ambitions to create a self-description of our own choosing. It is here that we select the seemingly most important path of our lives to date. Many Quarterlifers play tug-of-war between what they would *love* to do and what they feel they *should* do. Often, Quarterlifers are overcome by a fear to pursue their dream, particularly if it requires them to go against the grain. I suffered no small measure of terror when I decided to go for a career in writing, partly because it was so far beyond my safe circle of 'normal' options. That is not to say that all dreams are beyond the pale. Nor is it to say that so-called normal jobs are dull and dreamless. But I know too many people who hate their jobs, who settled for less than their passion, who played it safe rather than taking a chance, who were too afraid to ask what they really really wanted before rejecting other possibilities.

It's hard to be normal.

It's even harder not to be normal.

Easy come, easy go

We've talked about the multitude of options and expectations that aggravate the Quarterlife Crisis. We've also spoken about the rapid rate of change of the modern world, and the unique environment that that variability has created for Quarterlifers facing their present and future prospects. A by-product of these circumstances is the fact that change has increasingly become an acceptable state of affairs – even employers regard a degree of job hopping as normal. As Quarterlifers find their feet, they, too, have become more *au fait* with the possibility of change – indeed, added to the overwhelming number of options available is the option of change itself. It has become far easier to say things like 'If I'm not happy in this job, I can go and find another one'. While the chance to take charge of your life and to seek the ideal work or lifestyle environment is undoubtedly empowering, is there perhaps not a danger in change that is too easy? Let us consider divorce rate statistics: in many Western countries, two in three marriages are likely to end in divorce; and in the United States, people between the ages of 25 to 39 make up 60 per cent of all divorce cases[1]. It's really quite frightening. Perhaps it's a symptom of a world in which change is easier and where those who effect change most easily are Quarterlifers, the more adaptable, malleable and variable members of the population. And while the notion that 'nothing is forever' is particularly comforting when you're having a bad hair day or an argument with your boss, it is less reassuring when you enter a contract as sacred and serious as marriage.

But what does all this have to do with the dream crisis? Well, the point is that because effecting change is easier – sometimes too easy – we often don't stick things out anymore. The days of conflict resolution, at home and in the workplace, start to fade away in the face of 'irreconcilable differences'. It may also mean that we tend not to take the time or effort to discover our passions or exercise our dreams. We are the 'now' generation, demanding instant gratification and turning a slick 180 degrees if things don't go our way. Passions need to be nursed, and it's not always easy to locate or follow your dream. A bad day at work does not necessarily mean that you aren't cut out for the job, just as a tumble in your training does not necessarily mean that you aren't destined to run that marathon. Sometimes we need to take the time to get to know our innermost hopes, to massage our deepest aspirations so that they can break through the surface. Sometimes we need to sift through the worst aspects of a job before we understand that it *is* all we had dreamed it would be – it just took a bit of time to get there. For many Quarterlifers, then, the dream crisis is a crisis of not having a dream, or not knowing what your dream might be. But dreams take commitment – not just to find, but also to pursue.

Awakening

Quarterlife is, in essence, a rude awakening to the realities of adult life. In many ways, it would be so easy to stay behind in the safe structure of our school years, yet in other ways, we can't wait to get a head start on the future. Arrival at Quarterlife marks a realisation of some fundamental truths: we need to make choices and must bear the weight of those choices. At the same time, we begin to tackle some pressing specifics: we have careers to consider, homes to create, relationships to nurture, and selves to define. There may be a growing awareness of our accountability, to ourselves in particular. We need no longer depend on our parents or caregivers to set life's direction; this train runs on our own steam! Suddenly, dreams may become reality – if only we'd reach for them. And in this time of awakening we realise that with all the focus on becoming adults we may have lost that innate, childhood ability to mix a potion of passions. Of course, there's safety in building dreams as a child since a child is not really expected to go out and get them. But as a new adult, you have the chance to turn passion into living, breathing reality. And it's not so easy. For Quarterlifers, the dilemma around life's passions emerges as we question their validity, or even their presence. Suddenly accountable for our dreams, we wonder where they've gone. And so begins the search that is the dream crisis.

* * * * * *

I thought I was the only one to discover during Quarterlife that I didn't know, intrinsically, what I wanted to be. I thought everyone else had it all figured out and that, having chosen their course, they'd be content to stick with it. So when I started admitting that I was having a hard time identifying – let alone following – a primary passion in my life (let's leave my husband out of this), I was amazed to find that many of the Quarterlifers I talked to were having similar dilemmas. Like Tony, who left home after high school to travel, 'I thought I'd only be gone for a few months. It's now eight years later. I've spent the last couple of years in the UK, doing administrative support for any company that needed it. I'm sick of the boring office work and want to do something else with my life. But what? There are probably lots of things I could do but I'm not sure which I would love to do. I'm trying to figure out what would get me out of bed every morning, excited or inspired.' Or Nelly, a 28-year-old lawyer who resigned from her firm because she thought she'd be happier in a smaller organisation. Now she is finding it really difficult to find a new employer in a declining job market. 'I've been through grilling interview after grilling interview,' she said. 'I don't seem to say the right things or find the right companies. Maybe the issue isn't the size of the organisation or the type of environment. Maybe I'm just not meant to be a lawyer. But I can't even imagine being anything else; I come from a family of lawyers! Is this my life's dream? I'm not sure – it wasn't really passion that brought me to law – it was more like logic. And now I'm not convinced that is enough.'

SOLUTIONS AND SUGGESTIONS

Getting a handle on your dreams may well be like taming wild horses: treat them tenderly, and with loving attention, and don't be surprised if you get thrown every now and again. Like wild horses, dreams are tempestuous: although your greatest endeavour may be to capture one and make it your own, it will always have a glint in its eye and will occasionally strain at the reins. Horse whisperers would probably tell you that each animal is unique, requiring its own brand of care, and what works for one might not always work for all. It's the same with dreams: I can tell you how I came to find some of mine, but these suggestions are simply footholds on a rock face with many routes.

For me, the dream crisis was integrally connected to my career crisis. I have always wanted a career – not everyone necessarily does – and I wanted a career that was more than 'just a job' – most people usually do. I had read horrifying statistics about how up to 90 per cent of people are unhappy at work but simply resign themselves to it (rather than from it); I knew I didn't want to be one of those, but I didn't know how to harness a passion to take me out of that category. Moreover, other than my newly acquired husband, I didn't think I had any wild horses to tame – dreams seemed relegated to the bookshelves and Wham! posters of my childhood bedroom.

Coming to understand that I had a passion for writing and a dream of writing a book was a multipronged process: elimination (of careers I didn't want); discovery (of careers I might want); attention (to what other people were saying about my writing); conversion (of other people's opinions and my own hobbies into real-life possibilities); acceptance (of the fact that success is defined in many ways and that catching or achieving dreams is a long, hard process). I know that this is not necessarily my last stop on career parade. Perhaps I will tire of this passion, or perhaps it will tire of me; perhaps I'll find another, alternative dream that seems equally attractive; perhaps it won't suit the lifestyle changes that I am bound to make over the course of my life; or perhaps it will take up permanent residence. I don't profess to know; and I can't profess to not care – the idea of this not working out, or of having to start all over again with something new in a few years' time is not madly pleasing. But the sheer pleasure of having located a dream at all, and the propulsion of my own determination to at least try, brings some relief at the realisation that I must have the inner resources, even if I do have to repeat the process. Nevertheless, what follows are some needles and threads for you to use or discard at will as you embroider your own dreams:

Make your own acquaintance

Quarterlife marks the emergence of a whole new you, in many senses. As you surface, bleary-eyed, from college, an old job, or round-the-world travels, you face new challenges that will pressurise and elevate you in unaccustomed ways. Although you can rely on the strengths and resources that you've built over the years, you will also have to identify new ways of coping and be prepared to confront the world with a fresh face. To this end, those ancient Greeks and Romans knew what they were talking about when they advised you to *'Gnoti Seavton'* or *'Nosce te ipsum'* – Know Thyself. That ancient maxim cuts to the heart of one of life's biggest challenges. Obtaining a deep and abiding knowledge of your composition – physical, mental, emotional – is a daunting and rewarding task. Getting to understand what it is that builds, drives and excites you is ammunition in itself to tackle any crisis. Of course, there are countless books, therapists, websites and pop quizzes that can help you tread the wary path of knowing yourself, and what better time to start than the buzzing, ranting, question-filled days of Quarterlife?

I think of one Quarterlifer, Christine, a qualified and passionate doctor who always assumed she'd become a surgeon. But after some particularly harrowing experiences at a hospital, she had a real emotional shake-up and had to admit that she was not cut out for a surgeon's life. She was forced to re-examine what was best for her personality. Christine's realisation of her limits and her need to revise her life's path took many difficult months, but she slowly edged her way towards clarity. 'It's hard to think that I'm not the invincible rock I thought I was. I took some time off and decided not to go back to work until I had decided what was best for me. I've realised that my dream of being a doctor is still intact; it just got a little warped with my expectations of going above and beyond. I still want to practise medicine, but I certainly can't and don't want to be a surgeon. I just had to understand myself and reconnect with that deep passion for medicine to realise that there is more than one way to achieve that dream.'

Get to know yourself, and be honest with the answers you elicit:

What motivates you? Is it the desire for money, intelligence, lifestyle, love, status, revenge, peace, a corner office?

What excites you? Is it sports, books, electric wires, well-behaved children, poetry, public speaking, solitude, parachuting, sunbathing, balance sheets?

What bores you? Is it sports, books, electric wires, well-behaved children, poetry, public speaking, solitude, parachuting, sunbathing, balance sheets?

What annoys you? Is it politics, noise, large crowds, singing, exercise, fast cars, sycophants, the colour yellow?

What terrifies you? Is it speed, board-rooms, spiders, loneliness, heights, numbers?

What makes you laugh? What makes you cry? Who do you admire?

Who would you never let your children date? What do you want to say about yourself in 30 years' time?

Oh, these lists are far from exhaustive.

Expend time and energy on making your own acquaintance – despite how well you think you already know yourself – and begin excavating your dreams.

Dream again

I suspect it's far easier for dreams to wait quietly in the corner while Quarterlifers sort through the haze of coulds, shoulds or woulds incumbent upon us as newly arrived adults. But in the search for our life's passions and in the attempt to subvert the dream crisis, the identification of our dreams is paramount. So we actually need to learn how to dream again in order to work out what those dreams are and how to realise them. Perhaps we need to grab that hairbrush, don our leather jackets, and belt out 'Summer of '69' to the nonjudgemental silence of an empty kitchen; or stretch to the limit as we execute kick after kick of Jackie Chan-cum-Charlie's Angels martial arts against an unsuspecting continental pillow. Limber up the dusty legs of your imagination and get to know your dreams again. Choose your opiate: perhaps its free writing, or therapy, or the Inner Child cards sold at bookstores, or studying again, or meditation, or pottery, or fresh air … whatever will spur you on to dream. Find out what makes you interesting and unique – every one of us is. Be a kid again, in an adult's body.

Practical dream: A contradiction in terms?

I think that the adult tendency to stop dreaming becomes habitual the more absorbed we become in the physical world. As we grow up, and begin to assume responsibilities and plan our futures, the practical and daily become dominant, and dreams or fantasies seem too unreal to fit neatly into the sculpted lives we aim to lead. Social pressure forces us to consider the practicality and profitability of our dreams within strict constraints, and to discard those dreams that do not appear to conform. The need to excel, coupled with the modern generations' drive for instant gratification, means that 'passionate' often takes a backseat to 'sensible', and a dream becomes a mirage. But sometimes we need to consider the possible rather than the probable. Perhaps we wouldn't face such dream crises if, rather than asking ourselves 'can I make money out of this?' or 'what would my friends think if I were to… ?', we considered such issues as 'how could I make this idea feasible?' or 'what support structures would I need to put in place in order to make this dream come true?'. Just because they are dreams, doesn't mean they are unrealistic. Just because they are castles in the air, doesn't mean they can't have solid foundations on the ground. We need to try and subvert the peer and societal pressure that limits our life's work to checks and balances.

There's a big difference between a dream and a delusion. Is your dream realistic? With some forethought, motivation and planning, it is within the realm of possibility? Could you, with interest and dedication, make it workable? Try to find adequate ways to weave your passions into the need to be financially secure. Whether you pursue your interests full- or part-time, whether you turn them into all-consuming ambitions or nurse them on the side, try not to allow those interests to become tainted by material needs. Whether they represent the road to riches or not, they are worth maintaining as part of your life, at least in some measure. Can your dreams complement your work or even become it? Can you visualise your passions in actual terms and dust off the cobwebs to make them living, breathing realities? Then, as they say in the classics… just do it!

Look beyond the traditional

If you're having problems identifying what your dreams may be, perhaps you should widen the scope of your search. There is comfort in the familiar, and all too often, we set our sights on achieving or becoming things that we *know* of rather than what we *dream* of. At school, we tend to tailor our prospects according to the standard descriptions on the latest IQ tests: spatial reasoning + arithmetic capacity = a, b, c or d profession; social skills + ability to spell = e, f, g or h profession. Yet if you don't seem to be finding a life or work interest within those boundaries, perhaps it's because those options don't contain what's right for you. Look beyond the traditional. Be open to suggestions and opportunities that may come out of left field. The whole crux of the Quarterlife Crisis centres on the existence of opportunities – at times too many – but you would do well to use what the modern world has to offer.

Certainly, your mother and her friends may only have had the pool of teaching, nursing or bookkeeping to choose from, but yours is far larger, if only you would care to take a swim. Carve your own niche, if none seems to exist for you. Take chances, and, at all times, explore.

Can vs want

When I first started to panic about not having a dream or even an inkling as to what path I would follow in my life, I became fixated on everything that I *could* do: 'I can be a management consultant, I can be a psychologist, I can be a make-up artist (if only I can figure out the difference between blusher and rouge)'. It wasn't until someone asked me the question that I started to think about what I *wanted* to do with my life rather than what I should or could do. The two questions don't necessarily yield the same answer.

I think about one Quarterlifer's story here as an example: Burt was an outstanding academic at high school and followed the path that his family, friends and teachers supposed he should with his A aggregate – he applied for a degree in medicine. After seven long years of study, he graduated with absolutely no desire to practise medicine and went off to become a stockbroker, throwing expectation back in everyone's face. He fitted the bill to become a doctor, but had none of the passion.

And the opposite is also true: just because you love painting ceramics and could spend all day doing it, doesn't mean you should necessarily make a career out of it. They are the lucky ones – those whose abilities and passions conspire together to yield an obvious conclusion for their life's work. But most of us need to weigh can/should with want/love to find the right mix. I began to understand that just because I *could* become a manager in a consulting firm, didn't mean that that was right for me. For the most part, I had tended to focus on what my aptitudes and capabilities pushed me towards, rather than on what my interests and passions were showing me. I had to start finding the middle ground between can and want in order to understand how talents could become passions and how dreams could become reality.

Tell someone

The thing about dreams is that they're inside our own heads and hearts. They seldom see the light of day and rattle around our insides like Rapunzel in her castle prison. But the minute you verbalise your dreams – fledglings as they may be – and tell someone else about them, they suddenly have a voice. You know how saying something out loud often helps make it more real? If you've been fantasising about starting your own company or wishing to see the North Pole, spit it out. If you really want to stay home with your children or you've painted a picture you think is worth selling, say so. Telling someone else makes you accountable for creating, tending and achieving those thoughts, and makes it far more likely that you will go out and accomplish them. Articulating your ambitions helps to concretise them into achievable realities.

Of course it also raises the stakes and makes you confront the fear of failure: I didn't want to tell anyone that I had started a career in writing because if it all fell flat, then I would be the one to blame and I'd have to face the downfall of a dream. But I also realised that telling people about my new pursuit hardened my commitment towards it and helped build support. You can't expect encouragement from others if they don't know what you're up to. Once I told people what I was doing, I actually started to believe I was doing it. I thought that I couldn't call myself a 'writer' until I had had something published; but the truth was that I couldn't call myself a 'writer' until I called myself a writer – in front of someone else. And of course, as soon as I'd said it out loud, people started making the connections, referrals and suggestions that I could act on to help build my career, inputs which have been vital to my self-confidence and to the work that has been generated as a result.

At the same time, however, it is vital to maintain the courage of your convictions because not everyone you encounter will necessarily support your ideas or provide you with constructive criticism. Don't be knocked off your path too easily by negative critics. Hear what they have to say and decide for yourself whether it holds any value. Understand the motives for their response and use or discard feedback at your own will and prudence. But you'll probably find that most people will match your enthusiasm with their own. So if you have a dream, or suspect you have a dream, shout it from the rooftops – we're listening.

Dreams are hard work

I always envied those people who seemed so sure of what they were doing, as if things just fell out of the sky in a hailstorm of blatancy and wouldn't have worked any other way. I especially envied those people (usually actors and rock stars) who would say things like, 'What's amazing is that I'm getting paid for doing something I love'. Doesn't that sound like sheer bliss? But I learnt that (a) things aren't always as they appear so it's useless to envy people unless you really know their situation, and (b) being happy with what you do and feeling that you are living your dream is hard work. Not every day is perfect. I have horrible writing days, when words just won't come, and my motivation wants to stay in bed, and I feel completely frustrated and useless. I can pretty much guarantee that even Britney Spears has trashcan moments. (OK maybe crappy days are easier to cope with when you're 21 with a mansion in Beverly Hills, a smile that's whiter than white, and millions of fans who would scream and cry just to touch the piece of paper you stood on, but still...)

Passion, dreams, happiness – they all take hard work. How many hours of singing, dancing and abdominal crunches must it have taken for Britney to be where she is? We are quick to eliminate a potential dream for fearing that luck is too important a player in achieving it: you've got a beautiful face and want to be a model but 'you've got to be spotted, you know, and that's just lucky'; you have a passion for photography and would love to be a photojournalist, but 'you've got to be in the right place at the right time, you know'. One of South Africa's greatest sportsmen – golfer Gary Player – is famous for having said, 'The harder I practise, the luckier I get.' Touché. Hard work, that's what it takes. Guts, determination and staying power; the ability to pick yourself up from 100 rejections, brush the bird droppings from your jacket and start again. And as the star ice hockey player, Wayne Gretzky, so aptly put it, 'You miss 100 per cent of the shots you never take.'

If you want to get paid for doing something you love, then convert problems into challenges and hurdles into hassles. The world of dreams is not reserved for celebrities and heroes but for those prepared to go out and get them. And you know, sometimes you get paid a pittance – or you don't get paid at all – and you still can't believe just how lucky you are.

Dreams in practice

Here are some practical hints that may help you evaluate your passions and start implementing your dreams.

Set targets. Understand what you hope to achieve through your dreams and set milestones to assess whether you are any closer to fulfilling them. Your goals may be lofty, for example: 'In my career as a writer in the next two years, I would like to have written a book' or 'I want to climb Mount Kilimanjaro before I'm 35'. You may have smaller, nearer ambitions, for example 'I aim to write a chapter a month' or 'In my bid to be this city's greatest socialite, I aim to have at least one dinner party a week'. Ensure that your targets are ambitious yet realistic, and can be easily measured.

Set ultimatums. If you are unsure as to whether what you are doing is dream-worthy or if you aren't entirely fulfilled, set an ultimatum for however long you feel is appropriate to stick with it. Make that ultimatum long enough to achieve certain goals, but short enough to ensure that you don't get stuck in any ruts. Setting ultimatums is one way of ensuring that you constantly challenge yourself and assess your circumstances. You can keep regular checks on yourself by updating your CV every six months to track the changes in your life, honour your ultimatums, and monitor your goals. Not only is this useful in case you need to apply for a job, but also because your CV can act as a personal evaluation tool.

Get a mentor. Try to find someone whose opinion you respect in the matter of your type of work. Rely on this person for sound advice, good judgement and motivation in the pursuit of your dreams.

Find a role model. In whatever area your dreams lie, try and identify someone who has either achieved that same type of dream or whose own work you admire. This is the type of person on whom you might model your approach, whose style and manner you would consider emulating. This is not to say that you should 'copy' someone else and thereby lose your originality. It merely means that you can gain inspiration from other people's experiences and approaches to inform your own.

Build a support network. Surround yourself with people who encourage and motivate you. Interact with others who are on similar missions or in similar jobs, and build solidarity with a support network. For someone like me, this might be a writer's group or a writing course where I can meet others with similar interests and bounce ideas around. A support network builds confidence, offers a sense of collaboration even if your endeavours are singular, and provides a feeling of solidarity with others.

One dream, many dreams

In the previous chapter, we spoke about the possibility that you may have an affinity for more than one career, or have multiple talents. In the same way, you may have more than one passion or dream. Humans are multi-faceted beings, with numerous composite parts that make us as complicated and as troublesome as we are. Be aware that you may enjoy variety. Take advantage of

multiple talents if you have them, and try to find appropriate times in your life to satisfy one or all. I know a Quarterlifer businessperson who thoroughly enjoys her work but also sees herself in paint-spattered overalls one day, retiring to draw and sculpt in a garden cottage. She keeps up her artistic talents as a hobby while she pursues the business role that she finds challenging and rewarding. So if you find yourself grappling with more than one ambition, consider the timing and opportunities that are attached to them and appreciate the exceptional quality of being multidimensional.

Dreams on hold

If you're fortunate enough to have identified your dreams, hold on to them, even if you don't feel it's appropriate to pursue them right now. Circumstances sometimes require that we take care of other elements of our lives and selves, outside of our passions. Needs don't always conspire with desires. If that dream is important enough to you, then your obligation is not to lose sight of it. If you are working to place yourself in a situation whereby you may live your dream, then that is the pathway to the dream itself, and equally worthwhile. Consider Greg, who loves astronomy and studied it at university. But when he hit the big wide world, he saw other interesting options. 'I was given an opportunity in the dot-com world. I accepted the offer and that is where I still am. I'm in a management position, with lots of responsibility and freedom; I like the people I work with and I enjoy the day-to-day stuff. It's not what I always dreamed I'd be doing but right now there are enough uncertain variables in my life to deal with that I'm quite happy to have job security, and even job satisfaction. I think I've just put my first love on hold while I'm discovering a passion for this new area.'

With the luxury of hindsight, I can now see that my job in management consulting and the time I took to live and work overseas was vital life experience, without which my passion for writing may never have materialised. Nor do I believe that if I had started on my dream earlier, that my life would necessarily be any better off for it. I think that the key is not to forget your passions, even if you need to be doing something else. If you can't weave your dream into your life's work, then aim for a time that you may. Keep your dreams alive – asleep, but alive.

The dream is not the Holy Grail

Despite how I might have made it sound, having a dream is not about finding a Holy Grail that will signal the end to your search for meaning or answer all of your life's questions. Having a dream is about being passionate about what you do, enjoying your life's work and making the effort to optimise your experience of it. It's about aspiring to the 80/20 principle of maximum enjoyment and tolerable annoyance with your pursuits. You want to know what your passion is? Perhaps you're already living it. Think about it honestly. Is there another job or activity you'd far rather, realistically, be doing? Do you mostly enjoy your days and get pleasure from them? Just because every day isn't a picnic doesn't mean you're on the wrong bus. Don't get caught up in a ceaseless search for the perfect job or the perfect life when your own happiness, passion and fulfilment may be right under your very nose. If you are having a dream crisis (or fear it) use the crisis impetus to search yourself – your talents, abilities, interests, current state – and derive motivation from passion.

1 **Source:** The Divorce Centre, Inc: www.divorcenter.org

WHERE IS HOME?
[the location crisis]

As a South African growing up in the late- and post-Apartheid era, I have always been surrounded by 'exodus'. Friends, acquaintances, freedom fighters... everyone was always either in the process of emigrating or at least talking about it. Some left for political reasons, denouncing the separatist regime. Some left for safety reasons, fearing civil war and the rising crime rate. Some left for economic reasons, fleeing with a declining currency at their heels. Others were leaving because everyone else seemed to be leaving. As children looking to the future, it wasn't a matter of *whether* we would go; it was a matter of *when*. When democracy finally enlightened our sun-drenched shores, the pattern of departure was already firmly entrenched in the ways of our world – those who could afford to leave often did, fearing that South Africa would struggle to right itself amongst the woes of an already troubled continent. Many also stayed or returned, wanting to help build the fledgling Rainbow Nation, seeing opportunity and hope at every turn, or simply to reclaim a quality of life that was difficult to replicate anywhere else. But mostly, the concept of setting up roots elsewhere prevailed, particularly amongst my contemporaries.

My family was different in that respect. My parents are steadfast South Africans who, while maintaining an active travel itinerary and appreciating life beyond these borders, could not imagine themselves actually living somewhere else. While I was growing up, they certainly did not consider emigrating and had no grand plan for their family to set up shack anywhere else. They themselves were staying put, but would support whatever location choices my siblings and I might ultimately make. My brother and sister did take themselves off for postgraduate study in the United States; their motivation was to build new experience and knowledge, and they ended up staying in the US. I remained at home, happy in the new South Africa and even happier when I moved to that slice of natural wonder that is the fairest Cape. As a new graduate, my friends were all still around, my parents were firmly entrenched here, and although I missed my brother and sister, I was busy with my newfound independence. Since I felt no real compulsion – political, social, economic or emotional – to leave, I had no reason to contemplate it. I supposed I might go over and join my siblings at some point, perhaps to study or to gain that much-valued notion called 'experience', but I had no fixed plan just then.

Up to that point, the progression of my life had been neatly contained within the controlled structure of my student days, and my location simply followed suit. I followed a natural course of events, which ultimately happened to contain Cape Town as its backdrop. And since I was content to remain in South Africa at that point, there was no reason to rock the location boat. This was home; it required no explanation.

It was in this blissful haze that I started to notice a definite trend amongst my peers. Despite the constant ebb and flow of the tides which carried people from this country, I had somehow managed to remain within a circle of relative calm as far as these leaving issues were concerned – certainly my closest friends and most of my family were still at home. But, almost overnight, everyone seemed to be planning otherwise. Suddenly, 'London' was on everyone's lips, conjured up as an accessible yet sufficiently foreign perch where young adult birds could go to seek worldliness and experience (there's that word again). As if a great consciousness had suddenly swept my host of Quarterlifer contemporaries, every UK-bound airplane seemed to be filled with young hopefuls, looking to work in the UK and use it as a base to travel and learn. I was amazed. The rain-sodden streets and mould-infested rentals of this distant country seemed a far cry from the sunny climes and bursting exoticism of sunny South Africa. Why would any normal, Vitamin-D-loving African want to swap? But there was no doubt that going to London was suddenly the done thing.

To my further surprise, I found myself to be one of those caught in the London fever, thanks, of course, to Richard, a very convincing negotiator for the merits of foreign living, travel, and, no surprises here... experience. The risks appeared minimal, the rewards significant and the decision was eventually made. I hedged my bets and saw it as a big adventure that happened to involve living somewhere else for the time being. When I left for London, I fully intended to return to South Africa after a year or so. I wasn't saying goodbye to Cape Town. It was more of a 'Cheers, see you later; don't go making my road a one-way or putting up any prices, you hear?'

Chapter Two describes the sparks of the Quarterlife Crisis that flickered during my time doing 'the London thing'. One of these was undoubtedly the emergence of the location crisis as I began to realise that London was a halfway station for so many of the young foreigners who came there. I found a veritable melting pot of Australians, New Zealanders, Middle Easterners, Europeans, Americans... all of whom came to try their hand at London living and foreign travel. Yet relatively few of those temporary residents made their stay permanent. One friend remarked that living in London is about learning to say goodbye; people are always on their way somewhere else. For some, the stopover is longer, but foreign Quarterlifers living in London are inevitably faced with the question of 'how long will I be here?'. Some know their return destinations. Others are looking for them. For Quarterlifers who are already faced with the multitude of choices and decisions about their futures, the question of 'where to live' or 'where to next' simply adds to the fray. That's how it was for me. After a year and a half of living in London, Richard and I started wondering about the next step. Already entering the maze of questions about my career, my passions, my future prospects, I was also having trouble picturing where on earth my life's plan would play out. Reluctant to return home just yet, we decided to travel for a few months. But a new species of seed had been sown in my head, one that I had not expected to flower any time soon. I had changed my location status quo. I had made the move to London; I had experienced what it was like to live away from my home city – really, properly live, with floor mops and electricity bills and dinner parties for 15 in a matchbox apartment. I had made the break from South Africa, albeit temporarily, and succeeded. Without even being conscious of how I came to think such thoughts, I changed the question of 'when' I would return to South Africa to one of 'if' I would return. On the surface, nothing much had changed back home – I still had my apartment, my leave of absence, my telephone number, my faith in the country – but suddenly the concept of living elsewhere had become a real option.

As I looked around, I noticed friends talking about their next move. Canada, Australia, America. For some it was 'back home'; for others it was 'the next stop'. Were these places that I could consider? New Zealand, Europe, Hong Kong? My siblings were both in the United States, as was Richard's sister – wouldn't it be great to live in the same country as them again? Many of my friends were planning to go to Australia – perhaps that was an option? And what about London? I had enjoyed my experience there and felt almost entirely at home – maybe I should look at staying on? All of a sudden, banners were waving from all corners. My brother was enticing me to the US with promises of Hershey Bars. Friends were beckoning from Australia with letters perfumed by suntan lotion, and sprinkled with Bondi Beach sand. My parents spoke of the growing opportunities in South Africa and every conversation with them had the warm, familiar touch of home. New colleagues and friends in London promised nights on the town and an endless supply of Muller's Light Toffee Yoghurt (oh, the thought of it makes my mouth water) if only I would stay. I looked around the world and saw a familiar face in every corner. When did everyone get so split up? And how was I supposed to choose between friends and family, or opportunity and lifestyle?

What's more, it seemed expected of us not to return home. South Africans sometimes have a horrible habit of sabotaging themselves and their country by going elsewhere even when they would prefer not to. Yes, their reasons may be rational and logical, and their endeavours successful, but they leave their hearts behind. I kept getting the 'you're-young-and-adaptable-with-no-strings-attached-and-the-energy-to-make-things-work' lecture. Yet I hadn't really prepared to leave South

Africa completely, and all of a sudden it was a possibility if not a probability. But should I leave? And if so, where to? If I moved, how long would I stay in the next destination? When would I 'settle down', and where? And if I went back to South Africa – back home – would that be like admitting defeat, or declaring that I hadn't been able to 'make it' overseas? I felt bombarded by choices, and abandoned by answers.

WHY THE LOCATION CRISIS?

Although the location crisis is particularly pertinent to South Africans and perhaps for others who face insecurity in their countries of origin, it is not uniquely so. Modern living has evolved to convert the issue of location into one that has numerous possibilities. You may have many more than one 'home' in a lifetime, more than a single city or country that becomes your base for a period of time. The world today, the world that the Quarterlifer encounters upon entering adult life, is one where shifting locations mirror a transient nature of being that has become more commonplace. Young adults everywhere are confronted with a multitude of opportunities to live and work elsewhere. Particularly in the Western world, the cases of 'Dallas' Ewing-style living – where parents, children and children's children reside under a single roof for their respective lifetimes – number amongst the extreme rarities. In fact, in my experience, it is even unusual to find families all living in the same province or country, let alone the same town. Globalisation has shrunk borders and modern living factors the prospect of 'where' in amongst the maelstrom of issues that comprise the lucky packet of life and the Quarterlife Crisis.

It's a small small world

We all know the old cliché that tends to enter those conversations when

you realise that your new friend's brother is actually the boyfriend of your old Maths teacher's daughter. 'It is such a small world', you marvel, as you realise that the person sitting next to you on the airplane is the business partner of your sister's accountant. Travel has become cheaper and faster, making the world an infinitely more accessible place and promising to develop even more rapidly in years to come. Gone are the three-week boat journeys from Europe to Africa of my grandmother's era. Now you can do the trip in less than a day. Modes of transport are many and varied: cars that are fast and safe; buses that can travel long distances; trains that move at bullet speed; airplanes that have opened up the skies. I don't think an earthquake could have made my grandmother get up and move herself off to another place after the mind-boggling trip that she took to get to Cape Town. Yet picking up and laying down roots is no longer the logistical nightmare it once was, and the fact that one can cross time zones in a matter of hours has opened a well of opportunity to the worldwide population. For modern Quarterlifers in particular, who have grown up with this swiftly shrinking world and regard rapid travel as normal, the physical consideration of the travel element is a minor one.

As awakening Quarterlifers, we find that young adulthood presents us with the opportunity to not only visit alternative countries, but live within them as working and contributing members of society. Exchange programmes, working holiday visas, temporary and permanent residence permits... such notions not only facilitate cross-cultural experience, but also encourage it. What's more is that Quarterlifers in particular are often targeted as ideal participants: we are young, energetic, often skilled, unlikely to leech off the state since we can always get a job doing *something*. So the option of experiencing life outside of the familiar becomes a real and achievable possibility, and the easy ability to cross continents simply adds extra choice to a pot already boiling over with options.

Fax of life!

My cousin was recently having a discussion with her grandmother (on the other side of the family, so I can't take any blood credit for how much you do or don't laugh at this). She was telling her Grandma about her new computer, marvelling at its speed and usefulness for her university assignments.

'Darling,' said Grandma, 'I really don't want you spending too much time with that computer thing. I hear that you also use it to send messages to your friends and to look for information. Really, you must be very careful!'

A bit surprised, although used to her grandmother's customary cautiousness, my cousin asked, 'But why, Gran? You only have to be careful with something that is dangerous – why should I have to be worried about my computer?' 'Because, dear,' Grandma replied, 'I hear you can catch viruses from them.'

This story made me think about how technology has completely revamped the way we interact – with each other, with machines, and with the world. In fact, if I consider Grandma's literal take on the whole thing, the idea of a computer spreading physical infection is not so far-fetched if we think about how far we've come technologically, particularly with regard to interpersonal interaction. Mobile telephones, fax machines, e-mail, instant messaging, satellite communication... these are concepts that hadn't even graced the airwaves when our parents were still sending calligraphy-embossed love letters in the three-week post to each other. Developments in communication now facilitate the maintenance of international connections. More and more people find themselves faced with long-distance relationships as associates, friends and families move around the world. What all this has come to mean for the modern-day Quarterlifer is that you can, in some respects, be in more than a single place at once: I can be physically present in Cape Town, but engaged in a long conversation with a friend in London, finances permitting. And so the concept of living elsewhere is not unfeasible at all since you are still able to have some semblance of a relationship with those who are far away. Of course distance takes its toll – we haven't invented 'beam me up Scotty' apparatus just yet – but some of the impracticalities of living in different places have been abated through communication. We may not be able to catch a cold from our laptops just yet, but we can certainly send our love. So foreign living becomes even more viable and the Quarterlifer grapples with the option of multiple locations.

International business

As the world has changed, business practice itself has undergone massive renovation. Consider the impacts of travel. I can be giving a presentation from my office in Cape Town this morning, and still attend a meeting with colleagues in America tomorrow afternoon. Consider the impacts of communication: I can be giving that same presentation from my office in Cape Town today, including clients in Hong Kong and Australia amongst my audience via video-conference. Also, it appears that as businesses become more and more globalised, many of those businesses are adopting Business English as the prerequisite language of communication. In the context of the location crisis, this means that the choice of countries in which to work is greater than ever before. You need not be limited by physical attendance, ocean width, or even language barriers (though you'll still have to do your grocery shopping in the native tongue – unless, of course, you prefer online shopping for that purpose, too!) If you can use a keyboard, dial a telephone, and make yourself understood, you can pretty much pursue your work from anywhere, at any time. Like that grocery list, the catalogue of options regarding where to live grows by the minute as the world outside draws closer to our grasp. As eligible members of the world community, with the ability to learn and adapt on our side, Quarterlifers are forced to consider a multiplicity of options regarding where to live – because it's our right, because it's our luxury, because its our opportunity.

Worldly mentality, worldly expectations

Of course, it's not only the physical world that has changed so dramatically. People themselves have adjusted their perspectives to suit a new world-view. In particular, we have developed an increasingly more worldly mentality given our exposure to the world at large. Unless you are a farmer in an isolated rural area, or a monk on a lifetime retreat in the mountains, it seems difficult to maintain an insular or parochial approach to life. The world has an impact on us. We are forced to consider personal, national and international events in the girth of our own living space since international exposure, in all senses, is more common than ever before. To my father, it was a luxury to start up a noisy wireless and hear news from abroad while he was growing up; yet hardly a day goes by when I don't see international headlines on television. Markets, trends, friends abroad, imported clothing, exported fruit, globalisation… we can hardly turn a corner without having the world insert itself into our vision. In turn, expectations of how to live our lives have also changed.

Modern Quarterlifers may experience a feeling that one *must* leave home, let alone consider it. The Quarterlifer's perception is that, 40 years ago, families stuck together, travel was exceptional and short-lived, and the furthest away from your family you were likely to live was in a suburb across town. Now, not only is it common for kids to leave home at 18, but it is also encouraged as part of the maturation process. And once you've graduated, or worked a bit, it is fairly typical to travel the world. Leaving the nest, spreading your wings, tasting foreign life… these are now the ingredients for becoming grown-up, not to mention testing your worth. The Quarterlifer is young enough to adapt to change, fit enough to ignore jet lag, ambitious enough to take chances. We feel propelled to shake up our lives: 'I can get a working visa for a year in Italy, I should go for it – it's only a year. And after that, I can go somewhere else,' or, 'My parents never had the chance to be transferred to Vancouver, Chicago, Dubai or whatever other location my company operates in. It would be good for my career and I can always make new friends,' or 'It's not exciting just to stay at home forever; all my friends are moving around. I should get out there.' The world around us anticipates movement, whether we like it or not, whether we want to or not. To be young is to be mobile and that expectation is not always easy to bear.

Rootlessness

The ease of travel, the flow of communication, the internationalisation of business, and the worldliness of the modern mentality, have conspired to open countless doors to the corridors of the world. These elements have helped create a world platform that shifts and turns amongst the maze of flight paths, information super-highways and overnight express lanes which have undoubtedly made the world a more convenient place to be. Yet they have also created a growing sense of impermanence. When modern Quarterlifers contemplate the question of where to live, we are confronted by a transience that often causes discomfort. If we are so able to up and leave at the last minute, if we can live in a variety of different locations within a single lifetime, if we can have more than one place that we call 'home', then what does that say for the solidity of our lives? Where are our roots? Where do we belong? Together with enjoying the advantages of a more accessible world,

Quarterlifers must contend with a sense of rootlessness that comes with not knowing, with any certainty, that the place in which you happen to find yourself will always be your base. It is immensely difficult to lay down roots – of the adult and mature kind that Quarterlifers begin to consider – if you aren't sure where you'll be in five years' time, or even five months' time. Add a partner to the picture, who is also juggling location multiplicity, and the subject becomes that much more complicated.

Darryl is a 24-year-old Quarterlifer who is trying to fit his own location crisis into the fixtures of his girlfriend's life. 'Her family planned to go and live overseas, but they decided to go sooner than expected. Suddenly my girlfriend was headed in one direction and I wasn't sure where I was going. I haven't really thought about where I will land up living – I don't have strong ties to one place, and my work is portable. But I have to decide if I want to follow my girlfriend now and, if not, how long I can tolerate being apart from her. I feel too young to be "settling down" but at the same time, I know I can't wander forever – especially since I want to stay in this relationship. It's all so confusing.'

At a time in your life when everything else – career, relationships, identity – is being called into question, the location crisis exacerbates the situation because you may not have decided that this one place is where you will live your life. It denies you the physical solidity and permanence – the rootedness – of knowing you're 'home'.

* * * * * *

I hate to be crude, so please excuse me, but thinking about the location crisis makes me remember an old joke: Why do dogs lick their … um… undercarriages? Because they can.

Why do Quarterlifers often undergo a location crisis? Because they can. No previous generation has had the breadth of options regarding where to live as we have; no previous generation has been able to jump around the world with relative ease the way that we can. To some, this is a luxury. To some, it is a bind. To many, it is a crisis: of not knowing where 'home' is any longer, of the rootlessness that comes with too much wandering, of the discomfort that comes with always being the new kid on the block.

Quarterlifers are often bogged down by what they feel is the 'right' choice. Take Mel who lived at home with her parents until a study opportunity came up in another city. She moved, but she really misses her home, friends and family, and would gladly return. 'The problem was,' she says, 'I felt as if everyone expected me to leave home, telling me to go and live overseas, get a job and have new experiences. But I would have been quite happy just to stay put. I wasn't doing it for me – I was doing it for everyone else, or for what everyone else thought was right. But what's so wrong with sticking to one country or city and making a life for yourself there? Why this compulsion and expectation to leave home and move around?' It would be tempting to repeat the dog joke here!

Indecision

The coulds, woulds and shoulds of Quarterlife are enough to drive anyone south-west of sane. When I started grappling with the idea of 'where to live?', I felt really anxious – as if foundations were slowly loosening beneath me. I hoped that the time away travelling, with no work and supposedly no worries, would help me get clarity on the issue of where to live. But all my location worries only seemed to get further embroiled in a frantic internal debate which would remind me of its pressing need for resolution whenever I was (futilely) trying to ignore it. It seemed that no Tibetan monasteries, no Chinese chopsticks, no Vietnamese humidity was a match for the location crisis. As Richard and I wandered the world, it seemed to be demanding our attention. We ventured to Australia – essentially to see what all the fuss was about – and easily fell in love with the place. If you've ever lived in South Africa, it's not difficult to imagine yourself living in Australia with its warm climate, relaxed lifestyle, and friendly locals, and I could see why so many South Africans had chosen to make an alternative home for themselves there. I was almost disappointed that I liked it there. I had hoped that I would set one foot Down Under and hate the place, thereby eliminating one location option and making the decision easier. But it was not to be. At that stage, I didn't think that things could get any more complicated than they already were.

And then I got married.

Thinking as a couple

If I thought that dealing with my own location crisis was complicated, then dealing with both Richard's and mine was downright lunacy. Of course, we had been think-ing like a couple for quite some time already, but the fact that we were getting married made the issue of joint decision-making official – I couldn't very well decide to live in Cape Town while my husband was going to live in Timbuktu, no matter how modern a relationship we had! Richard brought alternative considerations to the party. While I had been primarily focused on where my friends and family were, Richard was also concerned with issues such as lifestyle and opportunity. He is a child of the sea, and of seaside living, only truly happy when there is a body of water nearby (lakes, dams and large baths occasionally suffice). He is relaxed and care-free, preferring the nonchalance of a coastal existence to the mad rush of city life. He has a passion for many things, and his work has taken him down different roads, so he wanted to choose a place that would be right for his career. Add all of this to my ups and downs about where to live, and you've got one mixed-up fruitcake.

We discussed our various options and couldn't come up with the perfect answer. We both love South Africa and had only viewed London as a temporary sojourn. We are both close to our family in America and wanted to live nearby them, yet our parents are still in South Africa and we wanted to be near them, too. We have close friends in the UK, Australia and America: these people are like family to us and we'd love to have them as part of our daily lives. Richard likes the lifestyle of a Cape Town or a Sydney and is happiest in those types of environments. There appeared to be opportunities in all the various cities, even a firm job offer in America (and anyway, we were determined that we would make our own luck, wherever we might land up). No place had all the answers. We were stumped.

We ignored the issue for as long as we possibly could – right up until our wedding day, in fact. (My brother's toast to us at our wedding hailed our 'brilliant if somewhat undetermined future'!). But it ultimately became too obvious to disregard and too immediate to put off any longer. So we decided to go back to the beginning. Neither of us had ever really intended leaving South Africa, but in the rush of Quarterlife and through the haze of our foreign experiences, we had somehow been diverted. We realised that we were simply juggling options without really understanding any of them fully. Of all the places we were considering, we'd only ever lived in South Africa and London. We had been to Australia once, on extended vacation, although we had visited it with the eagle-eye approach of evaluating whether it was a feasible living location. America had only ever been a holiday destination. It was clear that we needed to take a fresh, clean, honest look at the whole situation.

We thought we had enough information on South Africa, London and Australia to weigh them up at least semi-fairly. So we built the US into our honeymoon trip and went off to do a proper investigation of the places where our siblings lived, leaving the real treat – a Caribbean cruise – to the end in order to ease the blows of living the location crisis. Honeymoon over, we returned to South Africa, the one place in the world where we could lie low in order to collect our thoughts and make a decision – Cape Town, after all, was still home. It was there that we looked at all the location evidence, evaluated the various places as objectively as possible in terms of living potential, and took stock of the factors influencing us:

Friends. We were reluctant to make a decision based on our friends because we weren't sure how long they were all going to be in their respective places, and – to be brutal – friendships change over time, so it felt a bit hazardous to base a major decision on a factor that was potentially variable.

Family. Richard and I have both lived away from our parents and siblings for a long time and we were used it. So it seemed strange to envision them as part of our daily lives. We realised that family was more of a long-term factor, one that would become increasingly important as we grew a family of our own. But that itself felt so far off and difficult to comprehend right now, it was hard to really factor it in.

Lifestyle. Well, if that was going to be a driving force, then we really only had two choices: Cape Town and Sydney, since our siblings in the US live in cold climates and big cities, which don't really suit the surfer-life!

On and on the discussions roamed. But I think that the difficulty in making the decision to emigrate was rooted in one key issue: we lacked the impetus to move. We had both never really planned to leave South Africa, yet we struggled with the issues that seem to plague many young South Africans today: safety, economy, future, opportunity. The crime rate is a difficult issue, yet if you are living with it on a daily basis, you seem to cope — whether through desensitisation, or luck, or the fact that reality is rarely what the News makes it out to be. People worry about the economy and the sliding value of the local currency, fearing that even if they are able to maintain a good standard of living in South Africa, their earnings or assets will ultimately be worth very little outside of its borders. The future of the country hangs in the balance, as South Africa fights to correct the wrongs of the past and to blaze a trail through the heavy weight of the African continent. Young adults consider their prospects here and wonder where they are most likely to achieve their dreams, concerned that South Africa may not provide them with the opportunity or the exposure that another country might. Yet many other people regard these issues as secondary to the unique potential and quality of life that this country offers, preferring to see challenges rather than problems and to help build the bridges that will mark South Africa's crossing into the future. It's a cauldron of ifs and whens, buts and maybes... and the truth is that no-one knows.

My unexpected operation after our honeymoon meant that we were certainly not going anywhere for the next month or so. Richard found temporary work and I recuperated, still stewing over the right place to live. It was during a telephone conversation with a close friend who had emigrated that the penny dropped for me. I was discussing my situation with her and moaning about my state of uncertainty, when she offered the most blinding piece of clear logic that I had heard in a long time. She said, 'Jo, if you decide to leave South Africa, it must be for a really good reason, one that you entirely believe in. Because I can promise you that, once you leave, you will have some really horrible days when you'll have to remind yourself of that reason, when that reason will be the only thing keeping you in your new city – and if that reason isn't solid and your very own, then you'll always regret having left.' And that did it for me. I realised that Richard and I were beating ourselves up over this issue for all the wrong reasons. The pressure we felt to leave South Africa at this point came from outside. Other people thought it was a good idea; not us. The insistence we felt to make a move was being exerted by external forces: norms, expectations, hype, and not our own internal drive. I had begun to consider making a career change to writing, Richard was discovering a host of opportunities through his temporary work, and the option of South Africa was steadily becoming more concrete again. For right now, all the other possibilities were either wrong or impractical. The job offer in the US was far from ideal and was likely to cause more problems than it would solve; for the time being it was certainly no reason to move. Australia is horribly far from our family, and although it might represent a good long-term option, we had no way of securing entrance into the country at this time, so what was the point of stressing over it? London was an option born of familiarity rather than feasibility: it did not offer the type of lifestyle we were looking for, our friends were likely to move on from there soon, and renewing our visas would involve finding jobs we didn't want. Truth be told, Cape Town was still the option that offered the most answers.

So we decided to stop the location pressure. If I was going to change careers, I'd need a bit of time to get myself going. Richard was also keen to explore the opportunities he'd uncovered. We forced ourselves to realise that either our location decision had been made for us, or we had to put it off for at least another year or so. For right now, we were staying put – and happy to do so. If we had to leave again, or changed our minds in the months to come, then so be it. But for the moment, there was no need and there was no desire; without either, a change would be a dead loss. So we settled into the present. We looked at visa applications for alternative destinations, and hedged our bets, but concentrated on planting ourselves firmly on South African soil. Richard was determined that 'we should live here now as if we are going to live here forever. We must really commit to being in Cape Town – it's the only way we'll truly know if this is the place for us. If things change, then we will deal with it – we aren't the changeling generation for nothing'.

I still have days of questioning, when I wonder where I'll be in two years' time and I dread facing that location tug-of-war again. But I also feel that if I ever contemplate the decision of 'where to live' again, then it will be because I choose to. I have to believe that any future decision will come about because of a catalyst – my own catalyst – and that the location crisis I experienced was largely a function of expectation and perceived pressure rather than my own desire to change. I don't feel that sense of rootlessness anymore because I've decided that this is where I'm going to be for the time being and I've committed myself to making it work. For now, it's good to be home.

So I can't profess to have solved my location crisis. I certainly think I've mitigated it, though, and have set up some structures for dealing with it that will come in handy again should it ever re-emerge. You may find these suggestions useful, too.

SOLUTIONS AND SUGGESTIONS
Reality check: Options that aren't really options

The location crisis, like its mother Quarterlife Crisis, is often a crisis of options. Yet we tend to become bogged down in it before we fully understand the feasibility of the possibilities. Just because you may want to live in another place, or think that you have that choice, doesn't necessarily mean that you can. Consider that you still have to clear the possible hurdles that take the form of visas, finances, living arrangements, working arrangements etc., before you can even contemplate relocating. And some of those logistics might be difficult, if not impossible to transcend. For instance, what's the point of worrying about choosing between La La Land and Never Never Land if you can't get a work permit for La La Land, or if the yearly pollen count in Never Never Land is so high that your allergies could never tolerate living there? Think seriously about your options before panicking over them. Some ideas may be flights of fancy only – perhaps ones that you could act upon in time, but not ones that are appropriate (practically or emotionally) right now. Know when an idea is a diversion rather than an option.

Some fundamental realities may rule out options before they even become possibilities, rendering any anxiety that you generate in the consideration of those options a complete waste of energy. Furthermore, for the most part, preparation for relocation is a time-consuming process; it's generally difficult to up and leave tomorrow, even if you could pack in an hour. It's a rare case that would demand that you make a decision right this very minute (and if you were facing that kind of immediacy, you probably wouldn't be facing a location crisis). Take a South African Quarterlifer who has set his sights on Australia: unless he goes the more complicated or expensive routes such as getting a company to sponsor him immediately or having the big bucks to start a business, it could take a few years to put in an application and even then he might not be successful. So stressing about the option is futile until the option is actually viable. Use the lack of immediacy to ward off the crisis anxiety: you don't have to, in fact you probably can't, make a decision *today*, even if you wanted to. Try not to become anxious about options that aren't really options at all, and inject realism as a tonic to allay anxiety.

Identify, prioritise, negotiate

If you are struggling to come to grips with a location crisis and are starting to feel that all options offer nothing and no options offer everything, try to prioritise the considerations that are governing your decision. Identify what is important to you in the choice of where to live, and rank the elements in order of their significance or possible impact on your life. In my case, Richard and I highlighted the following criteria as important: proximity to family, proximity to friends, lifestyle, work opportunities, and safety. You might have different issues, such as: distance from parents (I have one friend who feels that he is better off in life when there is space between him and his immediate family); location in an area that is prime for your type of work; aversion to damp climates; religion; ethnicity… whatever the criteria are, understand what you require out of the place you wish to call 'home'. If you have a partner, get him or her to do the same process and compile your list together.

Check which issues are common to you both, and which are not.

Then try to sort those factors into a pecking order. Which are indispensable? Which are time-bound? Which are more important? This is not necessarily an easy process whereby the pieces slot nicely into their waiting positions. You may find that you and your partner disagree on the relative importance of Criteria 1 and 2, or that Criterion 3 ties with Criterion 6 in a race that can't seem to be won. Yet at the same time, you may find that issues you believed were crucial are in fact less so, or that the timing may be wrong to let Criterion 4 assume the front row position.

Understand which elements you can accommodate at this point in your life, and which may be able to wait, since it's not always possible to have everything at once and you may have to hold out for a future date to include some issues. For instance, in our case, Richard had identified lifestyle as one of his top priorities, but, after some thinking, felt that work opportunities should take precedence at this stage of his career. He thought that once his career was established, he'd be able to consider his desired lifestyle and try to include it.

Grapple with these issues until you feel you know them inside out. This process of analysis and sorting will help you to understand the elements that govern your life, and impose some sort of order in the chaos. It might not lead you to a foregone conclusion, but identifying, prioritising and negotiating your life's concerns will help create a structure within which you can tackle your location issues; and it will help eliminate the feeling that you are wading through the marshmallow thickness of a mass of options.

Research

As with any major life decision, the best way to go into the choice of where to live is with your eyes wide open. If you are eager to move, do your research. Get to know the prospects and requirements as well as possible. It may be tempting to follow the crowd, or choose a place for its perceived value only, but remember that this is going to be your every day, for however long, so you may as well have the best shot.

- **Get to know the place – ideally in person.** I couldn't realistically say whether I wanted to live in Australia or not – despite how many friends I may have there or how much I might love kangaroos – until I had actually visited the place and gotten to know it a bit. Of course you can't judge what it's like to live somewhere by what it's like to holiday there, but a visit will at least give you a first-hand impression that you can use to inform your decision.
- **Get to know what it's like to live there.** Talk to people who have lived there before or live there now, and get commentary about the way of life; decide

whether that will suit the priorities you've identified. Find out about work life, play life and standard of living. If you do visit, try to adopt an inhabitant's view as well as that of a tourist. Be honest, realistic and open-minded.

- **Get to know the prospects for going there.** Are there any visa requirements for your nationality? If so, what are your chances of being accepted? Different countries have different procedures for getting in, some stricter than others. Are your skills in demand? What are the job prospects? How long would it take to organise your move? What are the financial implications?

Know your cause

I must repeat my friend's pearl of wisdom that I found so useful in tackling my own location crisis. If you are leaving or moving, know your reason for making the change. Whether it's motivated by job prospects, financial prospects, fear for your safety, nomadic drives, whatever ... make sure that your core impetus is clear and worthwhile to you. Even if you regard the move as temporary, having a clearly articulated reason will help you navigate the change more effectively. And if the move is likely to be permanent, then knowing your cause can help make all the difference between a flutter of adrenalin and a full-blown crisis. Be honest with yourself. Make sure that your reasons are, in fact, yours, and not some desperate response to peer pressure or other people's motives. Because ultimately, when you're roaming the streets of your new location, miserable after hearing that a phone line will take three months to be installed, and the local grocer doesn't stock your favourite brand of coffee, and you read the statistics wrong so it actually rains 330 days of the year rather than 33, and you damn the infuriating devil on your shoulder that convinced you to make this stupid decision to move... then that underlying reason will be the critical driver that keeps you going.

Wait for the dust to settle

If you do move, then bear in mind that settling down takes time, isn't always easy and can place stress on your relationships. The fun and glamour of moving to a new place is joined at the hip with the uncertainties of starting afresh, the discomforts of not knowing the ropes. Don't expect to be fully integrated into your new life in minutes, days or even weeks. Although some people find it easier to deal with change than others, everyone takes time to adjust. Allow yourself that time. Make the requisite efforts to set yourself up, build your network and get to know things, but give yourself the space and time to let it all happen. Once you've made the decision to change locations (or even to stay where you are) and have set the ball rolling, then stick with it. It would be almost too easy to throw your hands up at the first signs of discomfort and head for the hills. Before you make the move, give yourself a realistic, and minimum, time frame within which to start getting organised: a few months, even a few years. Once you're there, set your mind on the task of getting settled and, if things don't start feeling better after that point, then re-evaluate. But not before then. Give the place a good six months to a year to seep into your bones before you discard it entirely. It probably took some effort to get you there, so make the effort to give it a go.

Trading places

While you're busy fretting over your location crisis, remember this: location, like many things, is changeable. It might not necessarily be easy or convenient to trade places, but it is certainly possible. I think I put a lot of pressure on myself by thinking that the place I choose to live next must be 'forever'. It took me a while to understand that the next place I choose to live must be right for the next phase of my life: marriage, career, family… whatever; it need not necessarily be the place where I grow old and plant my park bench. Of course it may turn out to be my ultimate destination, but I don't feel that that is really a decision I need to be making at my Quarterlife stage. I have chosen to stay in South Africa but if I find that something is drawing me somewhere else, then provided a change is feasible, I can move. Even with strings attached – like houses, cars, children – people manage to yank themselves up from place A and set themselves down again in place B. The Quarterlife goal is to try and root yourself in a place that will satisfy your needs, stoke your desires, and facilitate the achievement of your objectives; the goal need not be to find your final resting place. Rely on your adaptability to manage change. I think it's easier to deal with the location crisis if you try not to terrify yourself with the lifetime view; take things one phase at a time and make the decisions that feel right for your current and upcoming phase. Some phases are longer, and more 'mature' than others, but unless you are a confirmed psychic and can predict your future, then it's difficult to tell what your life will be doing 20 years from now. See Quarterlife as your mover-and-shaker years and choose the location which best suits your rhythm.

Have no shame

Perhaps as a result of its exalted position on the Top Seven list of deadly sins, pride is a factor that can often get in the way when making and breaking location decisions. There is nothing wrong with going home or taking shelter from the storm in a place that you know is safe. When Richard and I returned from our worldwide jaunts, I wondered whether our decision to stay in South Africa would be regarded as a cop-out. Would people think that we hadn't 'made it' overseas or that we weren't independent enough to live away from home? Despite the fact that we had never really intended to leave permanently, and stupidly allowing others' perceptions to affect our decision, I worried that it was somehow shameful to come back.

If I hadn't come back, I might never have pursued this passion that is now governing my working life. If I hadn't come back, I would never have witnessed the optimism, entrepreneurship and effervescence that bubbles, sometimes below and oftentimes above, this country's skin. I would have been ambushed by other people's judgement and allowed it to twist my fate.

You need to make the choices that are right for you – no-one else is living your life. If your chosen location turns out to be the wrong one, and you've given it every chance it deserves, then leave. If your location crisis brings you full circle, right back to where you started, then you're lucky – at least you already know where to get the best bread on a Sunday morning. If pride is the reason you're staying in a dead-end job, or maintaining a going-nowhere relationship, or sitting tight in a miserable city, then you're depriving yourself.

Let opportunity present you with choices, let realism negotiate those choices, and let instinct shape them. Let 'home' always be a sanctuary, whether it's a house, a city or a philosophy to which you return to regenerate. And let pride serve you only when you have something to be proud of.

AM I TOO OLD ALREADY?
AM I NOT OLD ENOUGH?

[the age crisis]

Recently, I went to watch the annual Schoolboys vs Old Boys rugby match at a local high school. Essentially, the game pitted the enthusiasm and macho bravado of the school's first rugby team against the brute force and look-how-much-we've-grown attitude of some older boys who return each year since their high school graduation to play this match. A close friend of mine was playing for the Old Boys and I went along to watch the fun. It was the first time since leaving my own high school, over a decade ago, that I have actually attended a school event, and I found it intriguing. It was filled with the stereotypical images of my mental yearbook. There were the preening teenage girls, all dressed up to watch a romp in the mud, waiting for the jocks to come off the field. There were the first aid boys standing by in their white jackets and surgical gloves, having resisted adolescent mockery to be on hand with ice packs and neck braces. There were the Geeks, the Dudes, the Goths, the Chicks, the Jocks, the Flower Children.

But what struck me the most was that they all looked so *young*! I was horrified. You know how you have a mental image of yourself at a certain age? And you know how you never seem to feel the age you actually are? Well, I think that in some recess of my deluded cerebellum, I actually pictured myself as close to 18. Of course, I have lived with the perks and pitfalls of being above the legal drinking age for some time already, but in my mind I didn't appear or feel much older than the kids who were now running around the field trying their utmost to look cool or disinterested. Sitting there at that sports game, watching the playtime antics of the guys and cringing at the high-pitched squeals and giggles of heavily lipsticked girls, I suddenly realised, with ice-cold clarity, that I was quite some way beyond wrinkle-freedom. I wasn't 18, or 20 anymore; I was on the wrong side of 21. I think that's what they call a revelation – or a horrible shock.

To be truthful, the idea of my chronological age has been niggling at me for a while. Over the past few years, I've had some experiences that have consciously placed age as a consideration, a hurdle or a benefit. When I went to London, people responded enthusiastically to the move, with comments such as, 'You're young – now is the time to see the world and move around before you settle down.' When my peers first started getting engaged, I would always wonder what the 'right age' was for marriage. Personally, I needed to be content that my age was sufficiently 'old enough' to be undertaking such a serious commitment. Next, a close friend, my age, announced that she was pregnant and I was overwhelmed by the feeling that we were too young to be having children – I still often felt 18, for crying out loud. Age became a subtle vein that could weave itself into even the simplest of decisions or fantasies: when Richard and I played the 'if you could have any car in the world, what would it be?' game, I would say that I'd never choose a Mercedes because they seemed more appropriate for 'older' people. Yet while I felt too young for a Rolls Royce, I felt too old for a BMX.

As my Quarterlife Crisis set in with its charming brand of vehemence, the issue of my age seemed to complicate matters even further. I wanted to see the world, but feared that my peers would 'outgrow' me. In the travel vs work issue, I became worried about starting or restarting jobs too late, and felt reluctant to be a beginner again. At the same time, when I considered a career in writing, I feared that I was too young to be taken seriously in such a field, and I wondered if I would be able to pursue multiple career dreams in my lifetime or whether choosing and committing to one now would eliminate the room for more later. And as for the decision about where to live, I kept thinking that now was the time to make the choice because I would quite soon become 'too old' to keep moving around. In some instances, I felt too young to be doing, saying, or deciding certain things; and in other instances, I felt too old. In very few instances, did I feel that I was just the right age!

My Quarterlife age crisis has been typified by paradox. My mental age still had me closer to puberty than midlife, yet I often had the strange feeling that time was running out. I felt a pressure to get on with things, to start setting up the very adult foundations on which the rest of my life would be based. The fact that I wasn't entirely sure which road to follow felt secondary to the need to be pushing, progressing, achieving. Wasn't 26 too old to be spending months travelling when I should rather be working on my career? I looked around at my peers who, presumably, were starting to establish themselves firmly, and felt a pressure to start laying down roots rather than experimenting and vacillating. But was I quite ready for a white picket fence and my own dishwasher? All those options out there might not come around again quite so quickly or easily – and I felt concerned about becoming too 'old' too soon. A close friend put it so well when she said, 'Quarterlife is about having acne and grey hairs at the same time.'

One of the most pressing age-related issues I've faced has been one that lies in that unique crossover between women and clocks. As I've moved closer to 30 than 21, and having recently married, I have become keenly aware of the expectation (particularly by my grandmother) that my logical next life step is to have children. I haven't really been aware of the tick-tick of my own biological chronometer, but it seems that friends and peers all around me are starting to bulge at the belly. Also, I keep seeing growing evidence of how difficult it can be to successfully fall pregnant without the trauma of fertility treatment or years of trying (you wouldn't think so when you're so busy slugging back contraceptive pills or sneaking condoms from public toilets). I realise that the longer I wait to have children, the more difficult it is likely to be. I realise that it's a blessing to have your parents, and even a grandparent, around to bond with your children and provide much-needed help. And my beloved grandmother, in her single-minded desire for more great-grandchildren, keeps pointing out that 'it's so lovely for children to have young parents'. I do realise all these things. But I still feel like too much of a child myself to have the responsibility of a little me or a little Richard. My dachshund puppy is enough. Quarterlife is filled with so many uncertainties and decisions that adding babies to the fray seems inconceivable! It seems that there's still so much to do before I could think about taking responsibility for another human life: careers to establish, homes to decorate, places to see, risks to take, mistakes to make. I'm physically old enough to have a child; I'm probably mentally old enough, too; but I somehow feel too young.

Too old? Not old enough? It's the paradox of Quarterlife.

WHY THE AGE CRISIS?

As human beings, we spend an inordinate amount of time wishing we were some other age. When we were kids growing up, we wished we were adults, free to pursue life without the boundaries of curfews, dress restrictions and 'I'll-tell-you-when-you're-21s'. When we hit Quarterlife, we hardly stop to realise that we should collect all those untold secrets now that we've exceeded 21, and we blunder about in the fog of either wishing for the structure and limits of childhood or fantasising about the supposed stability of 'real' adulthood. As 'real' adults, we bemoan our lost youth, unwittingly become those dreaded proclaimers of 'when-I-was-your-age', and spend our hard-earned Quarterlife money trying to rid ourselves of crow's feet. Yet while the rest of our lives is marked by a decided awareness of our age and what that entails – so no nightclubs at 14 and no skimpy bikinis at 60 – Quarterlife is plagued by an uncertainty about the expectations, demands and meanings of our current age. So while puberty or midlife is about 'I can or I can't', Quarterlife is more about 'should I or shouldn't I?'.

You guessed it... the technology boom

Any discussion on an element of the Quarterlife Crisis would not be complete without the mention of the technology boom. Together with the peaks and troughs of the information age has come a revised interpretation of business success and the age at which it can be expected. As boardrooms filled with youthful entrepreneurs, and hi-tech companies spoke to the young-at-heart, the possibilities for early success and financial gain broadened and Quarterlifers came to expect themselves to achieve a professional level which was higher, faster-paced and to be reached at a younger age than ever before. Despite the fact that the world is correcting itself of the technology overload, many Quarterlifers still retain that illusion of early success and early retirement. Now that the world has come to accept younger people as more viable and influential in the business world, youth is no longer the disadvantage that it used to be when pursuing a career or climbing the corporate ladder. Social expectations place a unique pressure on Quarterlifers to achieve at a relatively young age. It's no longer entirely uncommon for a 30-year-old to have already accomplished that for which his/her father worked a lifetime. This can create disappointment and dissatisfaction if the twenties and early thirties don't yield the professional or financial triumphs Quarterlifers have come to expect. They may feel left behind, or inadequate. It's almost a sense of 30 being 'too old' to begin a career or know your life's path; there's an impression that you should be well on your way by then and an unrealistic expectation of success. So the age crisis gnaws at Quarterlifers who are, in life's terms, still 'young', but who place on themselves the demands and expectations often more fitting to an older phase.

Age advantage

Modern generations in particular find that the Quarterlife phase is often regarded as a cut-off point for certain advantages in life. For instance, a working holiday visa for the UK is only available until the age of 27; emigration quotas favour those below 30 years of age as more viable candidates for acceptance; modern businesses regard younger recruits favourably as they are most likely to be computer literate and able to quickly acquire new skills. The sense that 'time is running out' becomes increasingly acute as Quarterlifers approach the end of the

20–35 age range and feel that doors are closing rather than opening for them. Inexorably linked to this is the fact that Quarterlife is, physiologically, the time in our lives at which we stop growing and start ageing. It's the first time that we look in the mirror and see evidence of lines around our eyes, the first time that sun-block becomes more important than a tan line. Paradoxically, of course, we may feel healthier, more knowledgeable and more marketable than ever before, but biology tells us that now might be the time to start joining in the search for the elixir of youth. At this time, we are pushed to think of ourselves in 'older' terms, beginning to focus more acutely on responsibilities and consequences. The age crisis emerges as we associate 'age' with 'ageing', yet still classify as, and receive the advantages of, the youthful portion of the population register.

Quarterlife = ¼ of the way through life

Quarterlife: the very term suggests an intimate connection with life's chrono-logy. And if 25 or 30 is a quarter of the way through life, then the total number of years we can expect to live is close on 100. Of course, the statistics are not always quite as hopeful as this, but the life expectancy of modern, Western generations is certainly higher than that of previous ones, having increased by some 10 years (from the mid-60s to the mid-70s as an average life expectancy) over the past five decades. This is largely due to the progress that modern science has made in fighting disease and illness; emphasis on a healthier lifestyle through exercise and eating well, and the promotion of good health, are factors which have had and will continue to have a marked impact on life expectancy. For modern generations, this means that we have more time in our lives to achieve goals, pursue interests and make our mark. In real terms, this should allow a greater time for each phase of life. And the concept of more time means that other options become available over and above the traditional linear flow from study, to career, to family, to retirement.

In contradiction with this idea, however, is the pressure that many Quarterlifers feel to move, push, achieve, and make inroads at an early age. Just because life expectancy is higher, does not mean that retirement age has been extended beyond the traditional 55 or 60. On the contrary, modern Quarterlifers, spurred on by modern business and modern opportunities, aspire to have achieved their goals (certainly their professional ones) by ages closer to 40 or 45. Quarterlife itself becomes the hotbed of both opportunity and paradox. Work now, travel later? Work later, travel now? Job 1 now, job 2 later? Job 1 now and later? Work now, marriage later? Marriage now, children later? And on and on it goes... In that itchy paradox of the age crisis, it seems that as we have gained more years in life, so have we become more afraid of running out of time. The Quarterlifer's tension comes from feeling simultaneously more and less mature, simultaneously pressurised to achieve at work and encouraged to take advantage of youthful, carefree pursuits. Acne and grey hairs.

Tying the knot and getting tied up in knots

As we navigate the 20–35 niche of modern life, we are faced with increasingly mature decisions and issues; and as we tackle the physical and emotional growth that befits our 'real adult' status, most Quarterlifers' thoughts inevitably turn to the concept of partnership and a long-term relationship with a significant other. Humans are amongst the few species that may mate for life – not that we always do, but we certainly have the capacity. For most people, Quarterlife marks our Initial Public Offering on the human stock exchange, the ignition of commitment to monogamy. Over the past years, marriage, or long-term commitment, has been slower on the uptake. From the 14- or 15-year-old betrothals of Romeo and Juliet's era, to the standard of marriage at 19 or 20 for my parents' contemporaries, to the modern-day preference for experimenting with single life and 'finding yourself' before finally committing to partnership in your late twenties or early thirties. Modern Quarterlifers tend to work on elements such as studies, career and travel before settling down, and the question of a long-term relationship often becomes mixed up amongst the turbulence of other Quarterlife issues. As with the practical advantages associated with life below age 35, the decision to commit to a single person makes us acutely aware of our physical age. If we are tempted to do so at the lower end of the Quarterlife scale, we are plagued with the question of 'am I too young?' and as we near the older end of that age range, we face fears of being 'on the shelf' or running out of time by becoming less eligible (generally a factor which affects women more than men, but still a consideration for both at some time or other).

Quarterlifers considering marriage or commitment often wonder whether they have done what they needed to do with their single years, given all the available, modern-day options. Being physically the 'right' age to find a partner and pursue a life together does not necessarily ease the confusion for many Quarterlifers who battle to define themselves, and can hardly imagine being committed to supporting and interconnecting with another when they themselves remain unsettled.

Children... the biggest decision of our lives?

The age advantage of Quarterlife and the contemplation of life partnership extend to what is perhaps the biggest decision of our lives – having children. There are few other occurrences that are likely to change our lives as irrevocably as a baby, particularly since it doesn't stop there: babies become toddlers, who in turn become angry pubescent teenagers, who in turn become young adults that will inflict on us their very own Quarterlife Crises! And it's not as if we can send them back to where they came from if we aren't happy with the outcome. Particularly for modern women, the 20–35 age range of Quarterlife represents prime baby-making time. The closer one gets to the 35-year mark, the riskier and more difficult it becomes to healthily conceive and bear children. Yet, as with the case of marriage or long-term commitment, women these days are choosing to have babies later and later. Where most women of previous generations had motherhood and family as their primary pursuits in adult life, many modern women are focused on building careers alongside their male partners. The choice to have children at an older age comes with its own price since a woman's fertility begins to decline after her mid-twenties. As a result, previously other-worldly concepts such as fertility treatment and surrogacy are increasingly commonplace these days as more women experience problems with conception and gestation. So Quarterlifers, hell-bent on taking advantage of modern life's opportunities, confused and sometimes disillusioned with the world they find waiting outside the hallowed halls of academia, and struggling with their identity issues, must add perhaps the biggest decision of their lives to this turmoil. I found myself contemplating whether I should be considering children, despite the fact that I did not feel ready, simply because I have become intensely aware of my physical age. I wondered if I should incorporate my one-day-far-away desire for kids into all the other plans I seem to be making now. The enormity of such a decision is not lost on me, though, and, like many other Quarterlifers, I feel the tug of physical, practical, age-related issues when I don't feel entirely ready to greet them.

* * * * * *

I was recently rummaging through a box of old photographs, and found a hilarious one of myself, age four, with my back to the camera and looking coquettishly over my shoulder, clad only in a navel-length t-shirt, my older sister's jewellery and my mother's black high-heeled boots. I looked at the photo and thought two things, firstly: 'This has horrifically embarrassing potential as blackmail so I should either burn it or put it in a safety deposit box', and secondly: 'Look how hard I was trying to be grown up; what I wouldn't give now for the innocence and worry-free life of being a child.' And that's the age crisis for you: stuck somewhere between the bare buttocks of childhood and the high-heels of adulthood, Quarterlifers belong to both and to neither.

SOLUTIONS AND SUGGESTIONS
It seems that the age crisis varies according to the advent of the Quarterlife Crisis. It's not about when you hit Quarterlife; it's about when Quarterlife hits you. For some, the crisis becomes apparent around graduation time when they face the big wide world of options, expectations and social reality; it is then that some Quarterlifers feel too young to be facing their very adult issues, almost wishing to retreat to the relative calm of childhood. For others, the Quarterlife Crisis plays its naughty game of knock-knock at a later phase, perhaps a few years into a first job or on returning from time spent travelling; it is then that some Quarterlifers feel the concern about getting started on a life path too late or falling behind their age group. For many, the event of turning 30 – which has long been renowned as a key emotional milestone in the sequence of life – heralds the emergence of Quarterlife Crisis-type issues: navigating options, negotiating expec-

tations, juggling multiple balls with a yet-undefined sense of self. For thirty-some-things, the age crisis is primarily a concern of already being too old to start afresh or a pressure to have achieved a certain amount by this stage. I include the 30–35 age range in the realm of the Quarterlife Crisis because I have found that some people in their thirties also face the Quarterlife career, passion, location and identity crises with the added pressure of age and the need to 'have all of this sorted by now'. Like the somewhat exceptional story of Anton who achieved professional success early on. 'By the age of 25 I had sold my company of 70 people for a ton of money and became a consultant, moving between different projects. Now I'm 31 years old and I've achieved what many people hope to achieve in a lifetime. People think that's glamorous and enviable, but to tell you the truth – I feel like I've missed out on the fun, social aspect of my twenties because I was so busy being a workaholic. Right now, my biggest goal is to find a partner to share my life – and that's no mean feat either. I know I've been lucky in some respects, and I've worked hard at my career, but I've started worrying about my age and what it means for life beyond my career. I almost want time to stand still so I can figure out what next before I get too old!'

The age crisis is often a crucial element of the Quarterlife Crisis because it brings with it all the social norms and expectations of milestones that underscore modern Quarterlife. Being one of the undeniably quantifiable factors in our lives, age seems to be a natural scorekeeper, the likely benchmark against which we measure ourselves and our achievements. We cannot change our physical ages, but we can change our responses to the age crisis. Yet I don't think the age crisis can necessarily be 'solved' in the way that the career crisis or the location crisis might. I think it's more about appreciating your current age, and conducting regular maintenance on your goals.

Ready, steady...

If the age crisis is causing you to feel undue pressure in certain areas of your life, ascertain whether you are in fact ready to face the issues being thrust on you. A close psychologist friend of mine is fond of saying that sometimes decisions don't feel right or comfortable because we simply aren't in a state of readiness to adopt them. I couldn't agree more. For instance, in the baby debate, I can't imagine that it's advisable to assume the mammoth task of raising children if you don't feel ready or capable. It makes sense that you have to be open and available to a concept in order for it to succeed, and the responsibility of becoming a parent is surely too immense to be undertaken out of peer pressure or a sense of age obligation. Nor can anyone else tell you how ready you are to meet your own challenges.

I met one Quarterlifer, Deana, who is 23 years old, married, and would love to have a child. But she feels as if everyone regards her as too young. 'When I've told people what I want, they often say things like "But you haven't lived your life yet" or "Wait until you've done all the fun stuff before you get so serious". But to me, having a family *is* the fun stuff. In my heart, I'm old enough to have a child, but in my head I think that maybe I'm not. My friends aren't having children yet, but I've had enough of partying and my job is not my life. Somewhere, there's this invisible sign-post that marks my social readiness to be a mother and people think I haven't reached it yet.' Your state of readiness is personal and unique.

Career is another path for which you need to feel the adequate sense of interest and commitment in order to make it work, and if you don't feel capable of such a commitment then perhaps you simply aren't ready for the task. I know one Quarterlifer who waltzed in and out of dead-end jobs for a few years after graduation before he decided to take some time out to pursue his interests of travel and photography. After eight months of seeing the world through a camera's lens, he finally decided to head home and commit to his career. 'I just wasn't ready before I took that break,' he said. 'I felt that this was just something I needed to do before I got properly settled in a job. Now I'm enjoying my work in business, really making a go of it, and building a good reputation. All it took was a few months of travel for me to confirm what I wanted to do and feel ready. I somehow didn't have it in me before that.' The same applied to my own situation: I wasn't even open to the possibility of a career in writing until I'd lived out other pursuits and allowed different possibilities to enter the foreground.

Perhaps the same applies to choosing a life partner. Quarterlifers start to feel a lot of pressure to find 'the one' and settle down. But if you aren't ready for that commitment, or aren't yet sure who you are, then it's unlikely you'll be able to conduct a successful relationship that is built to last. Nor is your own state of readiness necessarily in line with that of someone your own age who has a similar background; physical ages might be the same where mental ages differ. Readiness – for love, work and play – is like a fingerprint: unique to the individual. Know your state of readiness and use that as a foundation. Of course there is the possibility that some personalities never feel ready: some of us would 'play' forever if we could. But realities such as finances, biological urges or long-term visions can bring us round to a state of readiness and it is important that we at least evaluate them on merit. Ultimately, it's about understanding your own needs and having the courage to meet them or make them real. Be introspective, and honest with yourself; decide whether you are ready, regardless of your supposed age requirements, and take it from there. Set your own ultimatums and be your own timekeeper. Remember it's first ready, then steady, then go.

Moving goalposts

We've all heard, at one time or another, about how important it is to set goals. That's not to say that we necessarily all do so, at least not consciously, but there's no doubt it helps frame our objectives and gives us something to aim for in the future, whether in the short, medium or long term. But if there's one thing that I've learnt during this whole Quarterlife phase, it's that our goals often need to shift and change with the times; and that moving the goalposts is not necessarily an indication of failing to have reached them. The modern world is a mobile, fast-paced and ever-changing place. On that we probably agree. What that means to our goals – particularly ones that we may have set before we encountered the phenomenon and age crisis of Quarterlife – is that they need to be constantly reviewed and possibly revised in order to take changing circumstances into account. We've all had occasions of saying 'last year, I would never have guessed that this is where I'd be this year, or that this is what I'd be doing this year'.

Life is dynamic and it doesn't always make sense to hold onto goals that are unyielding or steadfast. If, at age 23, you had aimed to own three holiday homes on the European coast by the time you were 28 and, upon reaching 28, find that you can barely afford the upkeep on your studio apartment in town let alone a château and two villas, don't call yourself a failure just yet. Look at what you've experienced since the time you set that goal; understand how your life and the world around you may have changed and rebuild your goal so that it fits more appropriately with what you now know to be true. I'm not saying you should make unnecessary excuses for yourself, or not have lofty ambitions, but rather that you should take realism into account and ensure that your goals are achievable.

Take Salim, for example. He is a driven, motivated Quarterlifer who always wanted to be an investment banker. 'Investment banking is notorious for making sure that you have virtually no life during your first few years of work, but that you will make enough money in those first five to ten years to ultimately be very comfortable. And that was my goal, ever since university days – to be really good at my job, earn the salary and bonuses, and retire early. Unfortunately, the market took a steep turn for the worse, and the financial world became even more competitive and cut-throat than ever before. I'm not earning what I'd anticipated, and the working environment is really stressful. So now I'm getting closer to 30 and I haven't achieved nearly as much as I'd hoped. And I'm worried about getting old. It sounds ridiculous, but I really do worry about feeling like a failure if I haven't "made it" by 30 – that's the way my industry works! My twenties and early thirties were meant to be this big push for financial success, and now I'm not sure that I'll get there.' In Salim's case, conditions entirely beyond his control disallowed the achievement of his goal: rather than bemoaning his lost potential and feeling too old, he needs to revise his aims to suit the economic climate in which he now operates and take the age factor out of the equation. Getting stuck with old goals means getting stuck at the age you were at when you set them. Don't let age be your only judge of success or failure – things change far too quickly and unpredictably for that.

Start small

As a Quarterlifer, it isn't always that easy to set goals for five year's time when we can barely decipher where we are today. To lift yourself out of the age abyss and create some form for the future, start small: set a goal for next week, or six months from now. If you are the type who has never really set concrete goals before, and who only realises that you had goals once you either have or haven't achieved them, try writing some ideas down on paper. In all cases, be sure to keep your goals realistic and understand what you would need to do to achieve them. Monitor your goals like you would your cholesterol levels. Hold them in check so that you can swell and contract them to keep you realistically motivated and focused. Ultimately, your goals can play the vital role of ensuring that you understand your needs, play to your strengths, and listen to your passions. And most importantly, they help you keep up a constant dialogue with yourself.

Repeat: You are not old!

I've said it before and I'll say it again: you are not old! You may be nearing the latter end of the Quarterlife range, which makes you *older* than other Quarterlifers, but you're still not old. You may be fresh out of university and feeling pressurised to conduct yourself and your decisions with a more mature frame of mind; that doesn't make you old. Old is what your cheese gets when you leave it in last week's picnic hamper for too long. Old is what those gurus are who have already lived 100 lives in one. Old is what your mind becomes if you keep on saying that you're old. Think about it this way: if, according to some projections, there's a pretty good chance you could live to 100 or even beyond, and if life expectancy keeps growing year on year as it has done over the last half-century, then however 'old' you think you may be or feel, you're even younger than that in the grand schemes of science, technology and faith. Old is a state of mind. And state of mind is one of those precious human features that you can change.

BUT

You're no longer a child

You may not be old, but you're not a child either – at least not in that snivelling, mismatched, dependent way that you once were. Society emits criteria to proclaim adulthood: drivers' licences, drinking licences, voting licences. If you're a Quarterlifer, you're probably at or beyond those stage markers, which officially makes you an adult, whether you like it or not. There is a requirement that you start making bigger, more important decisions – not only because society says you must, but because as an adult you have the physical, mental and emotional capacity to do so. If you wish you could be a child again, think of all those things you'd hate to relive: wedgies, school bullies, summer jobs, 'I'll-tell-you-when-you're-21', getting your mom to drop you off at least one block from the nightclub. If you hated being a kid and couldn't wait to grow up, well then be thankful that you're finally here.

SO THAT LEAVES YOU AT...

A good age

Like a wine that's been standing for just long enough, Quarterlife is a good age. It often feels difficult, even insurmountable, but it does have a lot going for it. You can generally make changes without irrevocable repercussions, you can learn to adapt with relative ease, you can still transform bad habits to reap significant benefits. Although it might feel as if the world pushes and pulls you in various directions, your choices are ultimately yours and modern society does indeed accept that Quarterlife is an experimental stage. You are at the right age: for making decisions and changes, for testing the waters, and for plotting your future path. It's the mature 'learning by doing' phase of life, when mistakes are generally tolerated, if not encouraged; and it won't come around again. As a Quarterlifer, you are young enough to rebound and old enough to exercise judgement; you are young enough to mould and be moulded, and old enough to flex your wisdom; you are young enough to look young, and old enough to know what not to wear.

In the age crisis, we tend to fixate on being 'not old enough' or 'too old already' rather than relishing the fact that we are right in the middle. So perhaps one way to manage the age crisis is to realise that being a Quarterlifer has something to do with being a changeling. It places you on that fence between frivolous childhood and serious adulthood, when you can sift the best parts of both. If you liked the creativity of childhood, take up a painting class. If you look forward to the trappings of adult prestige, invest in unit trusts. Quarterlife gives you that rare window of opportunity to party at the club; or own the club; or both. Quarterlife is a mix of yesterday and tomorrow, and as uncomfortable as that may make you, understand that it is also a manageable and potentially wonderful time that is uniquely yours.

[the identity crisis]

The phone rang just as I was running out the door. 'Hello?' I breathed, now really late for an arrangement. 'Hi Jo, it's Eleanor.' I checked my watch – 6:05 pm. Officially after hours for my travel agent. Maybe there was a problem with our booking. Oh no, I thought; it's two days before Richard and I are due to leave on honeymoon and I know he's been furiously planning some surprise. I'd hate to have it ruined or postponed or divulged now!! 'Listen, I was just about to issue your tickets, and I needed to check what name I should put on yours.' Silence. 'Jo, you there?' What does she mean 'what name'? I only have one name, don't I? 'Hello? Jo? Should I use your married name or your maiden name from now on?' Swallow, gulp, breathe. 'Um, Eleanor, I'm going to have to call you back in a minute.'

I hadn't really thought about changing my name. Well, of course I'd thought about it in the dreamy, schoolgirl fashion of trying out a new signature, ages before Richard and I even contemplated marriage. But I hadn't actually thought about the practical implications of changing my name, let alone the emotional ones. I had no idea what I planned to do. I literally had no idea.

'Eleanor, I think you'd better leave the ticket in my maiden name. I haven't changed my passport or anything, so I may as well stick with what the official documents say.'

Richard came home that night to find me staring blankly into space. Scattered around me, like the mad sketches of a crazy scientist, was page upon page of signatures. Maiden name; married name; maiden-hyphen-married name; maiden initial-hyphen-married name... every permutation available had been scribbled and rescribbled countless times. And I was no closer to an answer. 'Who do you think I am?' I asked him, as he picked his way through the rubble to join me on the couch.

'What do you mean? You're you.' Cop-out!

'No really, WHO do you think I am? Am I my maiden surname, am I my married surname, am I a hybrid of the two? Who am I?' I was searching for an answer.

'You're whoever you want to be, my love,' he replied.

And thus began my deep-sea exploration into my own identity. I have been Joanne Jowell for my whole life. Was I suddenly meant to become someone else overnight? Just because I had signed a marriage certificate (with my maiden name, of course!) did that mean I was to automatically assume another persona as a Mrs? And never mind what I was meant to do; did I want to give up being who I've always been? Everyone knows me as Joanne Jowell, or some nickname derivative thereof. Who would know me as Joanne Something Else? I was having a hard enough time calling myself a 'wife'; changing my name seemed entirely beyond me. Oh, I debated this issue in my head endlessly over the next few weeks. On honeymoon, we were Mr and Mrs; any new person we met from now on in our lives would know us as husband and wife – if I took on my married surname, they'd never even know that I'd once been something, someone else. Besides, I liked being Joanne Jowell; I liked the alliteration; I liked the assumption of 27 years behind that name. Joanne Anything Else would have to be all new, catching up 27 years of personality, identity, history. I didn't want to have to start all over again at this age.

Round and round the issue turned in my head, driving me almost mad with indecision. I figured that if Richard and I ever had children one day, I would want us all to bear a single family banner. I wouldn't want them to know me as having one surname and Richard as having another. And I just assumed that that surname would be Richard's (call me a traditionalist on that one). So if that was the ultimate plan, then why didn't I just get it over and done with right away and start getting used to the whole thing? But what about my family legacy? I knew that my brother would officially 'carry on the family name' but what about all the meaning and the history associated with my own maiden name? I didn't want to lose all of that with one fell swoop of a pen. OK, then, how about hyphenating my maiden and married surnames to form one. Uugghh – much too long and unwieldy, plus that wouldn't solve the family-name issue one day down the line.

The more I grappled with the idea of my name, the more it started to bother me that I was now unsure of who I was, of my identity. Were Joanne Maiden and Joanne Married the same person? Would Joanne Married have the same close ties to her maiden family if she no longer bore their name? And as the issue wrestled in my head, it seemed to grow – way beyond the boundaries of surname. Who, in fact, was this Joanne person at all? Where did she belong? What made her 'her'? Like Alice tumbling down the rabbit hole, I felt like I was falling deeper and deeper into a chasm of not knowing who I was. My career was undecided, to say the least, and I was contemplating a complete shift into a work area entirely unknown to me. Before, my occupation had always comprised a large portion of who I thought I was, and now I didn't even have a distinct occupational title by which to refer to myself. It wasn't that I was just between jobs; I was between identities. On top of that, Richard and I hadn't yet made the decision to stay in South Africa, and the issue of where to live gnawed at the foundations of who I believed myself to be. I was a South African at heart, but an alien elsewhere. What's more, I now had this entirely new status of 'wife'; besides the name-change issue, there was the whole adjustment to marriage, mutual decision making and a renewed definition of us as a couple. So many of the things that I had become used to myself as being, were suddenly null and void: I was not a student or a management consultant; not a singleton or a girlfriend; not a resident of or a visitor to any place; not an achiever or a decision-maker. I felt like I was one of those annoying riddles that you play during long car journeys: I am neither here nor there, neither beginner nor expert; I am still standing, yet know not where I stand; I belong to no-one, yet I do not own myself. Who am I?

WHY THE IDENTITY CRISIS?

To ask 'why the identity crisis?' you need to look first to the concept of identity itself. Theses, tomes and bestsellers have been written on this subject, and more specifically, on the struggle to establish an identity at various phases of life: as infants separating from mothers, as teenagers trying to differentiate from the crowd, as midlifers acutely aware of mortality... I couldn't hope to encapsulate or even attempt to dissect the complex general issue of 'identity' here, and to profess to be able to do so is equally implausible. But a cursory look, at least, at the issue of identity is important for an understanding of the Quarterlife Crisis.

To be academic about it, we can look at the issue in terms of Oxford English Dictionary speak, where identity is (a) the quality or condition of being a specified person or thing, (b) individuality, personality. (I remember that my teachers used to take marks off in school if I started a speech or an essay with that old song and dance – 'The Shorter Oxford English Dictionary defines the topic as blah blah blah...'; I hope you'll be more forgiving here!) So in its barest form, identity is the frame we use to define ourselves, as individuals. Psychologically speaking, it is a person's own sense of self, their sense of who they are. As such, the identity crisis is crucial in the modern Quarterlifer's terms. Yet it may indeed be misleading to have broken it off as a single component of the Quarterlife Crisis because, in many ways, the Quarterlife Crisis *is* an identity crisis. The issues that 20–35ers face, when lumped together in a fumbling whole, amount to the issue of identity, since they address the composite of the self. All of those pieces can, in some way, answer the question of 'who or what am I?': a management consultant, an animal-lover, a South African, a 28-year-old, a wife... . The Quarterlifer's crisis is in trying to determine the choices you should make, and the elements you should tackle, to help fine-tune a revised definition of the self during a time of chaos and opportunity.

Changing times

At any time of change, the issue of identity is likely to shift – often uncomfortably – into the spotlight. Quarterlife is the quintessential time of change. So much is shifting: careers, relationships, friendships, interests, hometowns, wine appreciation, allergy tolerances... so many elements of life start to revolve as we make the move from student to adult, young adult to 'real' adult. Quarterlife is typically not a settled time, but rather one when the pegs are being staked out to form the outline of your adult life. It is a change of life phase that brings with it all the angst and searching incumbent upon such a process. With all this moving and shaking, the issue of identity must necessarily come to the forefront, since the questions that you deal with strike right to the heart of your own self-definition. If I change jobs, that means I'm a 'y' instead of an 'x'; if I change cities, that means I'm a 'b' local instead of an 'a' local. Certainly, if we regard those other elements of the Quarterlife Crisis – career, dreams, location, age – as its barest bones, then managing even one of those components and its own subcomponents is, of course, going to precipitate the 'who am I?' question. Each one of those pieces speaks to an aspect of how we see ourselves, and how the rest of the world sees us. Each one of those pieces helps to constitute the complex puzzle of our self-definition. Each one fills in the blank at the end of the various 'I am a...' statements that comprise the idea of 'me'. So identity is really the sum of the Quarterlife Crisis's parts; and the identity crisis is one that is initiated by change and necessitated by the complex round of life questioning that the Quarterlifer undertakes.

But as for the specifics...

Career

For the Quarterlifer, it seems that the identity crisis is often most closely linked to the issue of career. Although my own experience was of becoming aware of identity through a relationship/name-change issue, the question of career was undoubtedly not far removed. Career allows you to be a 'something' – it gives you a label, a title, a concrete way of presenting yourself to the world. When someone asks: 'What do you do?' or 'What are you?', the very questions revolve around the concepts of doing or being – life's essence, some might say. So career helps to define you in other people's eyes, and perhaps in your own, too. Further, given today's abundance of career options, Quarterlifers must have a thorough and intro-spective understanding of the self in order to make the right choice. Which career is right for me? Where will I be most successful, happiest and motivated? In career terms, Quarterlifers enter into a far deeper excavation of the self than generations before us ever had to, because the existence of choice and the perception of the need to succeed from early on, demand such insight. And when the answer is unclear, or the options are overwhelming, the identity crisis comes to the fore since not knowing what you do, or not being committed to what you do, throws a shadow on who you are.

I promise this is the last time... technology

Let's just take a brief look at the role of the technology revolution in the issue of identity. I've encountered numerous Quarterlifers who were thrown off their initial career paths by the lure of technology. Some found a happier niche in the computer world, but most others felt dissatisfied with what it ultimately yielded. As Quarterlifers, and along with the swan dive that the tech markets have suffered, they now face the question of whether the diversion to technology was indeed the right path for them. They begin to question whether their core identity suits hi-tech or whether they would fit in better somewhere else. Questions of passion, debates around 'is this what I really want to do?' and 'is this who I really am?' hark back to the core roots of identity. For these Quarterlifers, there is the fear of having misunderstood themselves and the crisis of having to revisit this aspect of self-definition.

Instant identity

Here's a hypothesis for you. Because modern Quarterlifers expect so much of themselves at such a young age, they barely have time to forge their identities as adults in the 'real' world before they are busy sprinting on the treadmill trying to reach their lofty milestones. There's very little slow progression in the modern world – it's all about pace and instant gratification – yet I don't think that identity is one of those things that you can whip up at a drive-thru. We spend years honing our identities as children and then as adolescents. We even have time to grow into our new selves as university students or young adults. But we feel the need to hit the ground running as the young, eligible, upwardly mobile accelerators of the human workforce.

I spoke to one Quarterlifer who felt this issue keenly. When Jenna was looking for her first job, she wanted to prepare for what she would say in interviews to prospective employers. 'I find the questions about my experiences or qualifications easy to answer because they deal with something that's quite concrete, but the introspective questions are difficult – questions about who I am as an individual and how I would describe myself. Since I've left university, I feel like I have to reinterpret the world. The 'me' that I know is a grungy, messy-haired student who goes to lots of Green Peace rallies. If I want to get a job and fit into the working world, I have to come up with or imagine the 'me' that I want to be and believe I can be – which is a whole different set of words! I don't feel like I know that person yet; she's still in the process of being born!'

Perhaps, as Quarterlifers, we have an identity crisis because we don't yet have an identity – at least not one that suits our new status in the world or takes into account the changes we face. In this case, the identity crisis isn't so much about not knowing who you are; it's more about not taking or having the *time* to find out.

Competition

Today's world is more competitive, and more aggressive than ever before. Viable candidates vie for often-limited jobs, tackling an increasingly competitive economic market and a demand for excellence. University degrees are no longer necessarily the coveted prizes they once were, as more and more students gain the opportunity for tertiary education, through classrooms that are both real and virtual. New training and development techniques and new approaches to management, mean that employers place an added emphasis on recruits having the right per-sonality, not only the right skill-set. Skill is generally seen as something that can be acquired while personality is not. What this means for Quarterlifers – themselves primary players in the whirlwind of competition – is that now, more than ever before, there is a need to sell yourself. To land a job, to find a life partner, even to be nominated for a volunteer committee, you will need to market your own personal brand to beat the rest. This requires a comprehensive understanding of what makes you 'you' and, in particular, what makes you unique. The pressure to find, polish and promote yourself hooks right into the question of identity, an often unresolved subject for many Quarterlifers who have yet to pinpoint the criteria which comprise their selves and set them apart.

Identity multiplicity

Part of what makes this brave new world so inspiring, yet so complicated, is the fact that you can be more than one 'thing' in your lifetime: multiple identities, so to speak. You can change jobs, marital status, hair colour, breast or penis size, names and addresses with relative ease, bearing testament to the remarkably variable nature of the modern world.

Let's take modern women for example: gone are the days when child-rearing and home-keeping were your sole expected occupations. Now you can be a chief executive of both your home and your company. Gone are the days in the Western world when you were regarded as your husband's 'property', and changing your name was automatic; today the surname options are numerous, reflecting equal partners in a modern relationship. The upside of this is increased flexibility, stimulation and opportunity. The downside is increased instability, indecision and difficulty in defining the self. For the modern Quarterlifer, identity multiplicity often means a splitting of the self – feeling your passions go one way and financial drives go another, or your friends go one way and your life partner goes another, or your career demands go one way and your maternal/paternal instincts go another. You worry about settling into one career when you might want to change cities later; or you worry about changing careers or cities and feeling rootless later. There is the sad suspicion that nothing is forever – that identities, like jobs or houses, may change. Is there a risk if you invest in building only one element of yourself? Is there any point changing your name for your husband if marriage is not guaranteed to last? I know

that's an awfully morbid viewpoint, but it is often part of the unrest that makes Quarterlife a particularly challenging phase. It's the possibility – and the plague – of multiple identities that pinches the nerves of Quarterlife and causes your head to spin with the manifestations of the identity crisis.

Relationships

One of the rudiments of Quarterlife change is relationships. At this point in life, they tend to become a lot more complicated than ever before. Friends start to move around, being drawn by forces beyond the confines of childish blood brotherhood or school ties. Like you, your friends may be changing jobs, locations, or marital status, and that means a shift in the way that you are used to interacting with them. You, the Quarterlifer, may start to look for different things in your friends, almost without realising it. You may relate to people on different – more adult? – levels and sometimes find your childhood or school friends unable to satisfy all your friendship needs. Romantic relationships also mature as you move closer to the realm of substantial partnership.

Professional interactions enter your sphere, increasing your span of relationships and introducing new vocabularies, exchanges and behaviours. Even existing relationships must take on the riptide of change that engulfs the Quarterlifer, and must adjust to suit a new, more mature order. Relationships are the means by which we interact, meaningfully, with the rest of the world – whether it's in person, on the telephone or via cyberspace. The changing nature of relationships during Quarterlife means an alteration of the way we relate to the world, and a redefinition of the self in respect of that change.

I was having a discussion with Richard who mentioned that, at this early stage in our marriage, he thinks I am still more of my parent's child than I am his wife. Let's not get into the issue of possession here, but rather look at how that observation points at my position relative to others, and at my Quarterlife struggle to understand which position applies most truthfully to my current phase. It's that 'relative to others' which is a shifting, yet critical element of Quarterlife. The need to redefine your relationships calls on the need to determine personal identity – very often the hot poker of Quarterlife's identity crisis.

Self-evaluation

Remember one of the most grisly parts of school – your report card? Remember the sweaty palms and minor heart palpitations at receiving the envelope containing your passes, failures and teacher's comments (assuming you cared)? Remember how much you simultaneously dreaded and longed for the arrival of that little demon? I never thought I'd miss the gut-wrenching process of receiving my report card, but I can honestly say that I do. I miss having someone else tell me how well or how badly I'm doing; I miss having regular feedback on my activities and capabilities; I miss being told that I can or can't, should or shouldn't. While I'm sure I reviled it at the time, I really do miss the structure and guidance of a report card. Because at Quarterlife – and for evermore – no-one gives you a gold star for a good job or meets with your parents to discuss your areas for development. If you have a formal job in a well-structured company, you might be receiving regular performance evaluations, but most of your life is now left up to you to appraise.

Quarterlife is the beginning of learning how to measure your own successes and failures, and of rewarding yourself for a job well done. You are, legally and emotionally, beyond the age of being 'not allowed to' and must become your own supervisor. It's a difficult task. It means understanding yourself, your potential and your weaknesses, having a firm grip on your identity, and obtaining the self-insight that will bolster you for the storms and let you ride the swells. No mean feat for the Quarterlifer who still hasn't even found the right job.

* * * * * *

I could probably spend pages waxing lyrical about the intricacies and delicacies of identity and Quarterlife's identity crisis, particularly since I believe that while some elements of the Quarterlife crisis are 'optional' – in that not every Quarterlifer who experiences the crisis will necessarily encounter each element, or each element to the same degree of intensity – the identity crisis is almost a given. Any time of questioning, any growth spurt or life-phase change, such as Quarterlife, is likely to introduce issues related to the catch-all of 'identity'. For some people, it's about their core purpose in life; for others, it's about the adjectives they use to describe themselves. For all, it's about the ways and means they use to sketch their own self-portraits and display them to the world. As Jim put it – himself a Quarterlifer struggling with his identity: 'Have the rules changed? Or is it just me? I still feel like a youngster, but the world doesn't fit so neatly into that view anymore. Or maybe it's me that doesn't fit. I feel as if I need to reprogramme myself.'

One step at a time

Jim's idea of 'reprogramming' is interesting, as it implies that you have a hand in creating your identity rather than being the passive recipient of the characteristics and quirks that conspire to form your self. It took me time to realise this.

I was still mulling around in my name-change swamp, no closer to having made a decision and with all sorts of stuff running marathons in my head. When we returned from honeymoon, and I felt forced to face the music, I had some heart-to-hearts with good friends. I have always been a big believer in two things as far as psychological issues are concerned, namely the value of therapists and confidantes. Talking about issues – really thrashing them out in the open ring of discussion – has always been one of my favourite pastimes, whether the issues are mine or someone else's. Never having been more open to suggestion than now, I listened with rapt attention to all the advice anyone was willing to offer me. One friend's solution was a simple, 'Down enough tequilas and you'll forget all about this.' But the hangover only increased the pounding in my head. Another friend threw my own advice right back at me, 'Have a long, hot, bubble bath; that'll help.' It did, but I had a problem – when I tried to write my name in bubbles, I couldn't decide which initials to use, and whether my handwriting should change with my identity. Another friend, who tends to rationalise if I emotionalise, finally planted the seed of solution. 'Do you realise how much you're dealing with here?' he said. 'Career change, dilemmas about where to live, adjusting to being home, changing friends, losing friends who have moved, getting married. Quite a lot, I'd say. You're asking a bit much of yourself to make all the changes at once, and feel happy with it. Slow down!'

So for the first time in my life that I can remember, I pressed PAUSE. I put on hold the endless drive to achieve, the constant need to know. I realised that I was grappling with more than a simple name or status change. I was dealing with the whole bang shoot of identity, laying the cobblestones for my future road. In this grand scheme, my name was only a name – a few arbitrary letters, strung together to form words that could pull me out of a line-up. Although I was assuming a different status as a 'wife', I was still me. The fact that I wasn't sure who 'me' was, had little to do with my name, per se, and more to do with the whole array of components that made that name meaningful – to me and to others. And working that out would take a bit more than designing a signature. If I liked me, Joanne Jowell, there was no reason I couldn't keep me. I just had to figure out what parts of me were up for discussion. And I sure wasn't doing that overnight.

I came to understand that my feelings of losing my identity had more to do with the fact that I didn't know what work I was going to be doing, and where I was going to be doing it, than with the idea of losing my surname. Now that my work was not cut out for me, I felt lost. For me, changing careers was like changing identity. Being married was not the defining factor, it just so happens that I got married at the same time that all my other Quarterlife questions came to the fore. I started to think about my own picture of myself, and of what, aside from my bodily matter, gave me presence. I have always been concerned with what other people think of me (perhaps overly so), and I used that perspective now to look at myself from the outside. I thought about the things that made me feel worthwhile, that distinguished me from and likened me to others, and tried to understand the pieces of my own puzzle. Joanne Jowell had held an identity comprised of multiple parts – work being a major one – and I now had to figure out whether / how those parts were going to change.

Like I said, I took my time with this one. I focused on my career and location decisions, and decided that my name issue could wait for the moment, since there was no pressing need for my signature on anything other than my credit card. I decided that since I liked my maiden name, and all that it represented to me, I would retain it as a second name if and when I ever got round to changing my name officially. And I decided that I would try out my married surname if and when I ever got the urge. I felt that I needed to live in tandem for a while – Joanne Maiden and Joanne Married – as I figured out the rest of me. So when it came to getting a local e-mail address (once we'd decided that we were staying put in Cape Town for the time being), I took out two – one for my maiden name and one for my married

surname, directed to the same Inbox – and left it up to my friends and correspon-
dents to decide which address to use. It amazed me how many automatically
started using my married one! And it's not as if the tone of their e-mails changed or
they felt reluctant to send the usual Spam to that address. They were still writing to
the same person; the name may have changed, the heart hadn't.

You may call this procrastination – and perhaps that's precisely what it is – but I
didn't want to rush the name process until I was good and ready. In fact, in some
ways, I wanted my inevitable adoption of my husband's surname to mark the point
at which I had figured out all the other Quarterlife issues I was managing; almost
like a graduation from Quarterlife, if I can be so hopeful. When people ask me what
I do, I still find myself saying: 'I used to be a management consultant, now I'm trying to be a writer.' My identity is still evolving – I'm sure it will continue to do so over
a lifetime – and my Quarterlife portion of it is in transition. But as soon as I have a
single piece of it worked out, as soon as I can complete another sentence of 'I am
a...', I bundle it up tightly and set it aside in a warm place to rise.

So here's what I've learnt over the past while about the identity beast, together
with some techniques that might be useful in moving through the identity crisis.

SOLUTIONS AND SUGGESTIONS
2 parts 'me' + 3 parts 'myself' + 5 parts 'I' = Identity

Identity is a composite. If there were a periodic table for psychological
concepts, identity wouldn't feature since it is not an isolated element.
Identity is made up of all the various pieces you use to describe yourself. This could
be work, marital status, religion, age, height, interests, ethnicity, personality traits,
likes and dislikes... .What this means is that everything you have ever been, and are
yet to be, forms part of your identity kit. The things that you were in your past may
no longer be predominant features, but they leave a residue on your identity in terms
of the lessons they taught you, the impacts they had on you, and the ways they
shaped you. It also means that identity is changeable as the various components in
your life shift. It is misleading to think of yourself as one 'thing' only; I feel that I used
to put too much stock in my classification of myself as a 'corporate professional'
which made it difficult to imagine myself as anything else, despite an intense desire

to change. So the question is how much emphasis you choose to put on one or more of those constituent parts... .

An exercise in priorities

Define what is most important for you to 'be' right now – is it your job, is it your relation to your partner, is it your status at the bank? Most likely, it's a combination of factors that you think would define you best. If you believe that you are going through an identity crisis, prioritise those components in order of personal importance. Ask yourself 'Which of the categories could I not live without? Which of those categories do I want to be best at?' To this, you will typically have an instinctive, gut response, and one for which it is important to be completely honest with yourself. For instance, I know that my work is, at this phase of my life, a priority; if I'm not doing something that I regard as worthwhile, I feel useless and valueless. I also know that my relationship is central to me; if I don't work on my character as a lifelong partner to Richard, I'll lose a part of who I am. But a few years ago, those identity priorities were different, and so were my impressions of what made my pursuits or priorities worthwhile. It's been a process of understanding the ranking of my identity ingredients, and how they've changed over time and through the Quarterlife experience.

The following are some 'identity exercises' that are fun, and quite revealing about how you see yourself. Try them out:

◼ Identity CV

Take a few minutes to sit down with a pen and paper, or do your workings in this book in the space provided.

Write out five nouns to describe yourself, as if you were writing an identity CV using only these words.

The words must be nouns or titles only (e.g. lawyer, husband, sailor, Catholic). Give yourself some time to come up with the list; sort through the various possibilities, either in your head or on paper, until you come up with the final five.

Rank the final five in order of importance to you: if you could only have one, which one would it be; if you could only have two, which would they be; and so on…

1 _____

2 _____

3 _____

4 _____

5 _____

Are you satisfied with the contents of the final list? Is there a glaring hole for an item you feel should be there but isn't? Would you change the list if you could? What would you do to change it? Were you unable to come up with five words / did you struggle to fill the list? The number here is less important than how satisfied you are with the list. What commitments can you make to either uphold or change the list as desired?

Ask a friend or someone you trust, to do the same exercise on your behalf, i.e. come up with five nouns they think best describe you. Are there major discrepancies between your list and your friend's? If so, why do you think that is the case? Do you agree with your friend's list?

And here's another one:
Take a few minutes to sit down with a pen and paper, or do your workings in this book in the space provided.
Think to yourself, 'If I were a fruit or a vegetable, I'd be a(n)…'
Write down what it is about that fruit or vegetable that best describes you,
e.g. *If I were a vegetable I'd be a pea, because like me, the pea:*
is popular (in fact the most widely eaten vegetable in the world)
likes to hang out in groups
is small and round

Think to yourself, 'If I were an animal, I'd be a(n)…' Write down what it is about that animal that best describes you, e.g. *if I were an animal I'd be a giraffe, because like me, the giraffe:*
has a long neck and long legs
is vegetarian
has a sharp kick when its angry

_____

_____

_____

_____

_____

_____

_____

_____

_____

_____

_____

_____

_____

_____

Read over what you've come up with and see how it describes your identity – look at both the physical and personality descriptions that come out of the exercise; compare the notes of the fruit/animal exercises, and notice any commonalities in the way you've described yourself.

Ask a friend / someone you trust, to do the same exercise on your behalf, i.e. come up with a fruit / vegetable and an animal they think best describe you and how so. Are there major discrepancies between your list and your friend's? If so, why do you think that is the case?

The characteristics that come out of these exercises can indicate the identity factors that are predominant or most evident in you and give you a baseline from which to identify / evaluate yourself and your identity components.

Don't forget:
Talking to a therapist or a willing friend can help you understand who you are, why you are who you are, and what you aim to be.
And of course, a bubble bath always helps!

Forming identity

We could probably get into some kind of a debate around whether you form your identity or it forms you, but I prefer a more proactive approach. If identity is a sum of your various parts, and you are an independent, thinking human being in control of your faculties, then you should be able to manage and mould your identity as you see fit. Of course, there are some characteristics that are impossible to change – such as your age or your ethnicity – but if those are priority components, then your task is to manage your approach to those aspects and to leverage the benefit you derive from them. It's almost too much to ask of yourself to 'define your identity'; but you can certainly define the component parts, particularly if you've prioritised those which hold the greatest meaning to you. So, for instance, figure out what work you want to do; outline your primary interests; decide what portion of your life will be taken up by religious or spiritual observance. If you're in the midst of an identity crisis, start your analysis with the parts of your identity that are easiest to identify. It's easier to think 'I need to figure out what job I'm most suited for' than to jump into the abyss of thinking 'I need to figure out who I am!' Here's that whole concept again of breaking things up into bite-size chunks so that they become less threatening and easier to manage. Sort through the various components that you feel represent you; try to understand how those components may change with time and circumstance; understand which are long-term fixtures and which are temporary; learn to balance, if you don't want one component to become too overbearing. The point here is to gain control over who you are – first by understanding your identity priorities, then by managing them. Begin with the most obvious elements and move deeper from there – there's more than just a single thing that makes you 'you', and only you can shape the pieces.

Role models

One thing that can help in the identity-shaping process is to find a realistic role model. Identify the type of, or the actual, person you would most like to emulate. Work out what it is about that person(s) you most admire / envy / aspire to become. It's not about pretending to be someone else, or wishing you were someone else (in that case, you're likely to land up more miserable than before since, in that existential clichéd way, we can never be anyone other than ourselves!). It's about pinpointing characteristics, behaviours and descriptors that you would most like to make your own – mixing them with your DNA means they remain unique, as individuals necessarily are. Think about how you can infuse those qualities into your own life and give them your own personal stamp of distinctiveness. Does it mean changing jobs, or finding a new interest, or accepting parts of yourself? Be realistic about your model, since this isn't about hero worship; it's about fashioning your identity components on an ideal.

I have a very religious friend who believes that, since man was created in the moral image of God, he should shape his personality around such moral characteristics. He uses religious teachings to exemplify the type of person he wants to be, and sets those features as his top priority identity elements, managing his life in accordance with the relevant principles and characteristics. He has his role model. Yours may be real or imagined, same sex or different, within your circle of acquaintance or not… the idea is simply to stimulate your own self-growth by having a clear picture of your ideal.

Transition

Quarterlife = change. And, as the old saying goes, the only person who likes change is a baby with a wet nappy. Your identity needs time to adjust to the mammoth transformations that are taking place in your life. It needs time to form itself around the shifting puzzle pieces that make it whole. Allow yourself time for transition and deal with only that degree of change that is manageable at the time – you don't want to blow your identity circuit. So my name change doesn't have to happen overnight; I use my maiden name when appropriate and test out my married name when that seems more fitting. The full transition will take time. During Quarterlife, we often feel bombarded by the sheer multitude of choices and changes occurring at one time; it's no wonder our identity gets into a muddle. Isolate pieces and work only on those that you can feasibly handle. If you're starting/changing jobs, getting married/divorced, having children/puppies, moving cities/countries, give your new identity pieces time to settle: say them in your head first, then out loud in the shower, then in cocktail-party conversation, as you get used to Quarterlife and beyond.

Quarterlife is almost a phasing in of a new you: there's no fixed time limit by which you must have reached completion. Parts of you will respond to that Newtonian law of inertia whereby they keep on moving even when you have stopped. You're a wannabee becoming an adult. You're a playboy becoming a father. You're a head girl becoming an ordinary woman. You're a caterpillar becoming a butterfly.

Walk before you run.

WHAT CAN I EXPECT TO FEEL? [emotions of Quarterlife]

One thing, amongst many, that has struck me during this Quarterlife phase is that there is a cauldron of emotion that seems to inhabit my mind (and often my stomach – I am a new inductee to the world of spastic colons and irritable bowels). Stick me in a childlike play-therapy group, and there is no way that the limited range of ☺☹😐 would suffice the way it used to. And of course, being an over-analytical fan of Psychology, I spend hours looking deep inside me and trying to chart my latest addition to the feelings barometer. It's not that these are emotions unlike others I've ever had – although some are, indeed, first-timers for me – but more that they seem to come unbidden at various times of the day or night, engulf me completely, and then beat a hasty retreat when I haul out my diary (to record them), my pyjamas (to banish them through sleep) or my husband (to lynch them with rationale). They are high and low; they are weird and wonderful. They are often mismatched.

Crises invite emotional responses. What follows is a description of the feelings that I have met during Quarterlife, and what other Quarterlifers appear to experience as well. You might find some more indicative of a 'crisis' than others, but the frustrating part of Quarterlife is that many of these emotions compete with one another and try to grab more than their fair share of a Quarterlifer's attention. It's that – the constant head-butting of emotion and the swirling palette of multiple intense feelings at once – which often makes Quarterlife a particularly difficult phase to manage.

THE DOWNSIDE

It goes without saying that many of the Quarterlife Crisis emotions hinge on the negative. Why else would we call it a 'crisis'? Although I have encountered a number of greatly positive emotions as well, it's primarily the negative emotions that require acknowledgement to ensure that they are managed and kept at bay.

Top of the list (although again, it's more of a plateau than a peak, with multiple 'tops' to speak of), is the feeling of **uncertainty** that most Quarterlifers have. I guess one can expect that a time of change be met with some hesitation or indecision. This feeling of uncertainty is exacerbated by the state of insecurity in which much of the modern world exists. There are threats to physical, economic and social security, in a world where terror and fanaticism have rendered even the most powerful countries vulnerable, creating a shaky surface on which we must live our daily lives. A sharp decline in 'the individual's capacity to create or restore his or her own security'[1] has rendered unstable the platform off which modern Quarterlifers now plan their futures. Multinational capitalism brings problems with opportunity; environmental issues threaten our planet; terrorists use the powers of modern communication and technology in deluges of fear. Who would have thought, a few years ago, that cellphones would trigger bombs or hijacked commercial airlines would be used as deadly weapons?! In fact, so serious is the issue of safety and security these days, that the United Nations has set up a Commission on Human Security to deal with such issues and their unthinkable ramifications. Certainly and sadly, our world is no bed of rose petals, and so modern Quarterlifers begin to contemplate serious thoughts and big decisions in the context of an insecure world, preying on their sense of certainty.

Furthermore, Quarterlifers dabble in excessive choice. They must, more seriously than ever before but still with the somewhat wild abandon of youth, weigh the consequences of their decisions, and may feel unsure of their next steps. Having left the structure and routine of childhood behind, the 'real' world itself is replete with uncertainty. Think of the example of a modern American supermarket and the variety of bread on offer. When all you want is a few slices to make your daily sandwiches, the existence of too many possibilities can cause less, rather than more, certainty. For modern Quarterlifers, their bread abundance is in the choice of jobs, careers, interests, pursuits, timings, locations, outlooks. It seems a treat to have so much choice; certainly, from the outside looking in, the Quarterlifer's Crisis of uncertainty may seem a luxury. Yet for those faced with an overabundance, too much choice creates ambiguity and sometimes extreme, and uncomfortable, uncertainty.

I actually did experience going into an American supermarket and trying to buy a loaf of bread; finding the entire range represented in multiple forms (white, brown, wholewheat, off-white, rye, sweet, sour, lite, light, sourdough, seed, seedless, nut, nutless...) and not convinced of the differences or my preferences, I would rather have run screaming from the store than have forced myself to make a choice. A couple of nights later, I had a dream: that I was drowning in a swimming pool of bread; every time I gasped for air, a loaf of bread – proclaiming to be the choice of choices – would bonk me on the head and send me floundering to the bottom. It's that feeling of being **overwhelmed** that clutches a Quarterlifer in its grasp and creates the sensation of gasping for breath. It's a feeling that leads you to believe it would be easier to ignore the choices and issues altogether than to face them head-on. This job or that job? This place or that place? And what about a third place? Don't forget that job. Appropriate or inappropriate? Older or younger? It's like a dose of emotional claustrophobia.

Look one way, you see one thing; look another way, you see another thing. That's the Quarterlifer's state of being. So for many, it's about being **in-between**. Am I a child or an adult? Do I enter the realm of serious responsibility (like career and family) or do I stay a while longer in the paddling pool of reduced responsibility that is still appropriate for my age? Should I plan for the short or long term? Should I choose a rock or a hard place, the devil or the deep blue sea? Quarterlife is about making a transition, and you have to ward against being caught in that changeover phase. It's about the jump from frivolous to responsible, from less to more mature, from variable to fixed, and underneath is a chasm of not knowing. Since the modern world demands an increased reliance on and accountability to the self, Quarterlifers may delay their assumption of a new role. Many perceive it easier to stay put than to inflict change, since the territory ahead is unmarked and unaccustomed. Often, there is a sense of being stuck, rendered immobile by the inability or unwillingness to change their current circumstances.

What further exacerbates this state of idling is a profound **nostalgia** for the past. With an uncertain future, Quarterlifers may ruminate on 'the good old days', missing the relative order and predictability of previous times. It's not uncommon to find a Quarterlifer staring longingly at the radio saying 'this song reminds me of that time when…' or glossing over the painful trauma of midterms and finals to reminisce about life as a carefree student. In contrast to the uncertainty of life in the 'real' world, school days were happy butterfly times when you knew where to go, and how to get there. But school or university didn't necessarily prepare you for the full onslaught of the world at large. So there's a sense of looking back to look forward, of missing what you had in anticipation of irrevocable change – and whether it's a change for better or worse is not the question. It's just that it's different.

Having to make decisions amidst uncertainty, getting stuck or unstuck, leads the Quarterlifer to an inevitable round of questioning. As life choices come under fire, Quarterlifers are often plagued by **doubt**. As they question their careers, or their homes, or their relationships, they also turn inwards and question themselves. Quarterlifers begin to wonder whether they are all that they assumed themselves to be. As the identity crisis becomes prevalent, Quarterlifers begin to doubt that which they believed to be true. They doubt their past and future choices, they doubt their own ability to make those choices, they doubt their skills and talents, their judgement and their stability. Here, there may be evidence of that 'impostor complex' – the feeling that 'pretty soon everyone will figure out that I'm not who they thought I was; I'm not as smart or as ambitious or as together as they, and I, once believed'. In essence, it becomes a crisis of confidence since 'all the rules are changing and who knows if I'll be able to play the game?'.

Questions of confidence, and doubts around your ability to make the right decisions, hinge on the risk that must now be taken. And with risk comes fear – in particular, the **'what if?' fear**. Quarterlifers can spend aeons playing the scenario game. What if I have chosen the wrong career path? Would I have been happier or more successful doing something else? What if this is the wrong person for me? What if I waste time? What if this job actually has no impact or relevance? What if I delay having children and then find that I have problems later? What if I fall behind my peers? What if I never find my passion? What if...? There is an overriding fear of making a mistake, born of the impression that consequences are becoming more serious, and of the often erroneous perception that everyone else has things sorted out by now. Feeling the pressure to figure it all out and get going, Quarterlifers contemplate risk in a new and untapped manner, and fear the out-comes of the wrong moves.

Nor does it feel like there's a whole lot of time to make those moves. I know that I have often had the feeling that I'm running out of time, that although I'm supposedly still young and adaptable, I nevertheless need to get cracking. This sense of **haste** is quite difficult to manage in its juxtaposition to the mammoth depth and breadth of decisions that must be made during Quarterlife. You would almost prefer to have time to weigh the options and plot the potential. Yet due to perceptions of social expectation, self-imposed pressure and the modern rate of change, Quarterlifers feel pushed to hurry up and make it happen. Never mind that they might not know what 'it' is, there's no time to waste

in finding out. Quarterlifers enter their own little race – against contemporaries, against time, and against norms – since this phase of life is perceived as optimal for climbing grown-up ladders. This is the time to work out all the big answers to all the big questions; there is no more time for dawdling. This emphasis on finding meaning – and finding it fast – pushes the envelope for some Quarterlifers. I'm thinking here of the stockbroker who quits his job after five years to travel to Thailand and teach English, feeling that his work on the trading floor will never truly impact lives. Or the shining young business consultant who leaves a promising career to become an adventure travel guide. Or the 29-year-old guy who, having gone out with his supposed beloved for four years, breaks off the engagement two days before the wedding because he's now 'not sure'. The impetus to quickly find life's meaning may cause some Quarterlifers to turn their lives upside down in order to ensure significance. After this, according to the Quarterlifer's take on things, you'll either be too old or too settled to stoke the fire of momentum, so you may as well 'make haste while the sun shines'!

When and if the Quarterlife Crisis hits, 20–35ers often experience some **loneliness**. This isn't necessarily a physical loneliness (unless you've taken yourself off to the outer reaches of Antarctica in a bid to live it up before you're too old), but rather an emotional sense of isolation. Many school friends will have moved on or changed, social circles become social squares as peer groups shift, and the individual Quarterlifer is forced to become more self-reliant than ever before. In the bid to define the self there is a movement away from the common room and common psyche of the past; you can no longer gather in school halls or count hundreds of your closest friends on the lawns of campus. Perhaps you've moved to a new city or have started a new job, necessitating new friendships that require hard work; even maintaining your existing relationships takes a more concerted effort, despite how close you may be, since you now have private homes, schedules and priorities that don't always accommodate the easy drop-ins of before. There's also the possibility that you feel your life is changing in a different direction to your old peers or friends, growing a silent wall of weeds between you. Relationships must be reshaped to suit the change in life phase, often leaving the Quarterlifer longing for the easy cliques of the past.

And then there's the emotion of **disappointment** when you realise that you can't have everything. Your job might take you away from your friends or family. Your changing priorities might mean that you leave your home country behind but can't take your parents with you. The feeling that you're 'getting old' might mean that you swap your thrill-seeking adventures for life-preserving ones. And there's the feeling of disappointment when you realise that maybe the big wide world isn't all it's cracked up to be: that there's a reason they call it 'work'; that receiving lots of envelopes in the mail is more indicative of your impending bankruptcy than your undeniable popularity; that having the freedom to go out on a 'school' night simply means you'll have to set two harsh alarms for the morning (and probably still have to ask your mom to call and make sure you're up on time!) Hitting Quarterlife, or being hit by it, is a cold shower in the face of childish anticipation – it wakes you up, but not always to the sound of music.

For some 20–35ers, Quarterlife is a hard knock – harder still since they don't feel entitled to complain or verbalise their concerns because they're supposed to be having the 'time of their lives'. In such cases, the emotions we've spoken of in this chapter take on painful proportions and life can become difficult to manage. Most Quarterlifers reach a point where questions about the future become more and more pressing, actually forcing resolutions and ways out of the crisis. In some cases, however, resolution seems impossible; the extremity of emotion may become too much to handle, and symptoms of **anxiety** or even **depression** can set in. Before we go any further on this subject, let me say that such symptoms can be varied and often have a physical and a clinical basis. We're not talking about feeling a little worried that you won't get your dream job, or a little down because you're struggling to make a decision about where to live; such concerns are ordinary and common. Instead, we're talking about the psychological, classified conditions of anxiety and depression, which are complicated, treatable, and may have their roots in issues far deeper than the Quarterlife Crisis. Yet the Quarterlife Crisis may indeed be a catalyst or a cause for such conditions and the possibility thereof must not be overlooked.

We'll get to the known symptoms of anxiety and depression in a little while, but let's first look at how the emotional, Quarterlife-specific components may manifest in the case of anxiety and depression. Essentially, I think these are exacerbated versions of the trademark Quarterlife-Crisis emotions. **So:**

THE EMOTION OF	BECOMES A FEELING OF
Uncertainty	Insecurity
Feeling overwhelmed	Inability to cope
Feeling in-between	Being lost
Feeling stuck	'Leaden feet' / being unable to think clearly
Doubt	Extreme mistrust of self and the world
'What if' fear	Extreme pessimism, self-sabotage and anxiety
Haste	Panic
Nostalgia	Mourning
Loneliness	Being abandoned; wanting to isolate yourself
Disappointment	Distress

Underlying these emotions is an inability to foresee resolution to the crisis (not necessarily knowing the resolution but rather lacking the capacity to imagine that there could be such a thing) and unwillingness to try.

From a clinical point of view, the symptoms of anxiety and depression are well documented. It is important to note that you should not attempt to self-diagnose such conditions. Doctors and specialists are equipped to identify symptoms of anxiety or depression and help treat them. Therefore the details contained in this book are for informational purposes only and should not be utilised for diagnosis. Any suspected anxiety or depression should be evaluated and managed by a medical professional.

Anxiety and anxiety-related disorders are an extension of the natural 'fight or flight' response that humans have to danger. If you're a caveman and you encounter a wild tiger, your body releases hormones which enable you to either tackle the beast with your opposable thumbs and superior intellect, or run for your life. These fundamental responses are associated with physical symptoms that result from the rush of adrenalin, such as a quicker heart rate (so that your brain, lungs and muscles can get blood faster) and quick breathing (to increase oxygen levels). So your body naturally prepares to fight or flee. However, in the case of anxiety and anxiety-related disorders, your body is unable to distinguish an anxious thought such as 'what if I fail?' or 'should I really be doing this job?' from a physical threat such as your common and garden tiger. Your body cannot tell the difference between a thought originating in your mind or in the outside world. An anxiety response keeps the fight or flight response going in a loop, so that it doesn't allow you to calm down rationally. You experience emotional/mental symptoms such as: panic and fear, obsessive thoughts, sleeping difficulties, lack of concentration and extreme exhaustion. Physically, you may experience such symptoms as: nausea, sweating, muscle tension, rapid heartbeat, breathing problems, shaking and dizziness. Of course not all symptoms are necessarily present at one time, nor is the presence of one symptom necessarily indicative of an anxiety disorder.

There are numerous types of anxiety disorders, not all of which share the same symptoms: panic disorder, where the primary marker is a panic attack; phobias, where there is an intense and irrational fear of a specific object, activity or situation which is then avoided; obsessive-compulsive disorder; post-traumatic stress disorder; and generalised anxiety disorder. For all of these, the fundamental issue of concern is the inability to rationalise or avert the anxiety response, an issue that can be successfully managed through treatment.

Depression, like anxiety, also has suspected roots in genetics and physiology, and its diagnosis and treatment are best handled by medical professionals. Most of us, at some point in our lives, have said, 'I feel so depressed', yet the manifestation of clinical depression is far different from, and more severe than, a feeling of being 'down in the dumps'. A Quarterlifer experiencing full-blown depression will experience a persistence of the negativity and hopelessness which they feel surround their life-change issues, and is likely to be suffering from some of the following: overwhelming and unrelenting sadness or unhappiness; feelings of being helpless, worthless, pessimistic and / or guilty; substance abuse; exhaustion; loss of interest in ordinary activities; irritability; problems with eating; sleep disturbances; increased crying, anxiety and panic attacks; difficulty concentrating or making decisions; thoughts of or attempts at suicide. Once again, this list is not exhaustive, nor does the manifestation of one or more of these symptoms necessarily indicate clinical depression. However, if you suspect that you or someone you know may be depressed, it is vital that professionals be consulted. One of the major issues with depression is the reluctance to talk about it. Despite modern advances, a progressive society, and research pointing to the physical roots of depression in brain or chemical imbalances, many people still stigmatise depression and feel that it is an indication of weakness. So admitting to depression, or the possibility thereof, is difficult for those who don't want to display such a 'fault'.

The need to recognise and treat depression is made even more pressing by the growing incidence of suicide amongst young people. Statistics amongst the Quarterlife age group, and even younger, point to an alarming suicide rate, which appears to be on the increase. The World Health Organisation[2] reports that, in the last 45 years, suicide rates across all age groups have increased by 60 per cent worldwide and although the rates have traditionally been highest amongst elderly males, rates among young people have been increasing to such an extent that they are now the group at highest risk in a third of all countries. Theories for the increase in suicide are many and varied, but one factor that does seem to be widely acknowledged is the pressure under which today's youth find themselves: academic pressure, peer-group pressure around drugs and alcohol, pressure to find a good job, pressure to gain financial status…

these are the tough by-products of our fast-paced, modern world.[3] Depression itself – which, like many mental illnesses tends to make a first appearance in teenage or Quarterlife years – is a leading factor associated with suicide, and it has been shown that suicide is more likely to occur during a period of individual crisis. So the overlap between depression and the Quarterlife Crisis is a potentially fraught area, the gravity of which should not be underestimated.

Treatment for depression depends on the evaluation that a professional makes, and can be approached in a variety of ways, including medication and psycho-therapy. These are some suggestions as to what you can do for yourself if you are indeed suffering from depression:

- Since you are likely to feel that everything is an effort not worth making, focus on the small things. Don't wait for a bolt of lightning to strike and to wake up one day miraculously 'cured': give yourself one or two small tasks to accomplish each day (from getting dressed, to taking a few deep breaths outside, to doing the grocery shopping). Build on them slowly until they don't feel like such mammoth endeavours.
- Refrain from taking on too much responsibility or work at this time.
- Prioritise responsibilities and only do as much as you can manage.
- Try not to expect too much of yourself too soon, since your life is not operating at its usual pace. Being overly demanding of yourself will unnecessarily increase your feelings of weakness or failure.
- Although you probably don't feel like it, try to be around other people as much as possible. Socialising is an effective way to manage your mood and will stop you from ruminating too much. So go to a movie, have coffee with a friend, or take part in religious or social activities that you may enjoy.
- Exercise! You don't need to overdo it – even going for a short walk, or doing some deep breathing is effective – but you must make sure that you help your body to build physical strength as much as you are able. Further, there are known psychological benefits since exercise releases endorphins, the body's own pain relievers that are associated with feeling happy or good. Do not exercise if you are physically unwell (e.g. have flu or a virus), but remember the physiological and psychological benefits of keeping fit.

- Give yourself time; depression doesn't go away overnight.
- Refrain from making major life decisions while you are depressed, such as leaving town or quitting your job. These decisions might well be beneficial at some point, however they should not be taken without consulting your doctor or psychotherapist, and others who know you and can advise you well; and they are certainly best left until you are out of the woods.
- Remember that depression is the reason you may be feeling worthless, exhausted and as if there's no light at the end of the tunnel, so try to keep a handle on your pessimism. Such negativity is part of the illness and is not necessarily a true indication of your circumstances. In the midst of depression, it's a bit difficult to see the bright side; but the negative thinking is likely to pass with treatment.

If you're a concerned friend or family member of someone who is depressed, you may not be able to understand why that person isn't able to just snap out of it. It can be very frustrating to try and remain sympathetic when you don't feel as if the depressed person is doing anything to help him/herself. Try to understand that the condition is not solvable by a simple 'don't worry, it'll all be OK tomorrow', or by my favourite 'have a hot bath' remedy. The condition is a complex combination of emotion, physiology and circumstance, so it will take some time to abate. In the meantime, you, too, can help:

- Encourage your friend / family member to get professional help for diagnosis and treatment; you may have to do some handholding to get them there.
- Make sure they know that you are there to support them, no matter how much they might sound like a broken record. Be realistic without being judgemental of their feelings. Show affection and patience, despite your frustration.
- Encourage the person to socialise and go out with you (but don't push the activities). Keep it simple – like going to the movies, or for a walk in the park, or out for lunch. And encourage them to take part in hobbies or activities you know they usually enjoy.
- Keep an eye on the future. With treatment, the depressed person will get better; keep reminding yourself, and them, of that.

It is vital to never ignore talk of suicide by a depressed person. In particular, be wary of the following danger signs:

- Statements about worthlessness
- Statements about feeling helpless and hopeless
- Preoccupation with death
- Loss of interest in the things they care about
- Suddenly happier, calmer
- Suddenly visiting or calling people they care about
- Making arrangements, setting affairs in order
- Giving things away

If you suspect that your friend or family member may be suicidal, contact a doctor or psychiatrist immediately.

Further information on anxiety and depression can be obtained through literature (local libraries, bookstores), Internet websites, mental health organisations, social service organisations, family doctors, hospitals and mental health professionals.

THE UPSIDE

All this talk of negative emotion is enough to make anyone depressed. And the truth is that Quarterlife is also replete with a range of positive emotions, which tend to be ignored in the context of a crisis. Like the rest of life, Quarterlife is about navigating both the highs and the lows, so we should not overlook the positive emotions often associated with it – in fact, we should probably strive to focus on them.

Every now and again, I know I certainly get a flash of breathless anticipation. Despite raging against the uncertainty and doubt of Quarterlife, there is also the sense of standing on the brink of something potentially wonderful. As much as Quarterlifers may miss their past and appreciate it more in retrospect, they also have the knowledge that Quarterlife itself can be a time of freedom and opportunity. Decisions may be hard to make, but they can also represent a whole new outlook on life that you simply weren't ready to adopt before. This kind of realisation – often unconscious – inspires a unique feeling of hopeful expectancy for what this phase of life might deliver.

Sometimes, Quarterlifers lift their heads from the muddle of options that bombard them, and feel **appreciation** for the hive of potential that they are indeed privileged to negotiate. There's something about being part of this new world that you cannot help but marvel at it, particularly when considering how much has actually changed in our favour over the last few decades. Yes, these are changes that have stirred such a thing as the Quarterlife Crisis – undeniably a complicated time – but they have also brought with them whole new realms of prospect and possibility. Democratic rights, women's rights, technological developments, business revolutions, attitude transformations… these are leaps and bounds from which Quarterlifers are fortunate to profit. Amongst the chaos of it all, lies the seed of opportunity.

So you call your friend overseas, who conferences in your other friend living in another country so that all three of you can join in on the same conversation. You go to sleep on one continent and wake up the next morning on another, just in time for your early morning business meeting. You sync your handheld personal organiser to your laptop and your mobile phone so that you can always have that friend's telephone number at hand just when you need it… and you think to your-self, in a moment of **wonder**: I'm actually pretty lucky; 30 years ago, my parents would have waited three weeks to receive a letter from overseas friends, by which time all news was old news anyway; and my grandmother took those same three weeks to travel from one continent to another, sharing cabin space with those old-news letters; and even ten years ago, my hand would ache at the end of each day from writing all my appointments in the diary that contained my whole life and would really distress me if I lost it. It's amazing to think that in 20 years' time, my days will be the 'olden days'. Things change, and it's not always such a bad thing.

With this recognition of the uniqueness of your place in time, comes the Quarterlifer's feeling of **vitality**. The age-crisis dredges up questions of whether the Quarterlifer feels closer to 'old' or 'young', but the ultimate realisation must lead to the understanding that you still have energy, vigour and statistics on your side – you are 'older', but hardly 'old'. In the gulf of Quarterlife dilemmas, there is at least a fleeting awareness that it is your vitality that allows change to still be feasible and facilitates the existence of options. Without it, you would not have the means or the might to even consider the issues that face the Quarterlifer – yes, there's still some immortality fantasy left in you!

The paradox of Quarterlife lays uncertainty down in the same bed as anticipation, nostalgia with appreciation, haste with vitality. Quarterlifers may have none, all or some of the feelings reflected in this chapter. For the most part, they'll refrain from talking about it to others since they don't attribute those feelings to the grand make-up of such a condition as the Quarterlife Crisis. In fact, perhaps one of the most common feelings is that of being **alone**. Not 'lonely', but rather of having no commonality with others since you find yourself in this strange and unaccustomed phase which must surely be unique to you. Certainly, when I first read of the concept of the Quarterlife Crisis, my first response was 'So I'm *not* alone', having never stopped to contemplate that perhaps there was an entire generation of people out there experiencing something similar. Going through a Quarterlife Crisis is nothing special; knowing that you're going through a Quarterlife Crisis is.

1 **Source:** *Weekend Argus* (South Africa), 'What To Do About That Uneasy Feeling', 14 September 2002,

2 **Source:** http://www.who.int/en/ ; http://www.befrienders.org

3 **Source:** C. Wallerstein, 'Unbearable Burden of Life', *Guardian Weekly*, March 14–20 2002, 25.

SOLUTIONS [but not conclusions]

I'm standing at a bar in town, trying desperately to ignore the fact that I swore I wouldn't come back to this same place, with the same people, on yet another Saturday night. Richard is standing next to me, bemusedly rolling his eyes when another of the regular crowd shuffles in. 'Didn't we promise we'd go somewhere new this week?' he jokes, knowing that we'll always return to this place where we're guaranteed a good time. 'I think we're too old for this,' I say, although I'm not entirely convinced since there appears to be an astounding contingent of over 35ers here. A friend, one of the new ones I've made since returning to Cape Town, comes over to chat. 'How's the book going, Jo?' She settles onto a barstool, getting ready for the weekly chapter-by-chapter low-down. 'Solved your Quarterlife Crisis yet?' 'Don't be silly,' I laugh. 'These things don't get solved; they just get lived.'

It's almost dangerous to use the word 'solutions' when it comes to the Quarterlife Crisis, since there is unlikely to be any one thing that can put an end to it. Yet solutions are what people are inevitably looking for, particularly since Quarterlife can seem so devoid of the finite decisiveness that the word 'solutions' suggests.

I prefer to think of *managing* the Quarterlife Crisis rather than *solving* it, because I don't believe that the crisis is necessarily time-bound. It doesn't appear one day in a rush of symptoms and then disappear a week or so later once you've slugged the right tonics and done the necessary amount of soul-searching. It is more typically an ongoing state of being that may require multiple approaches to tackle the various issues. If you've read this far, and have found some of this book applicable or simply recognisable, then you've taken the first step towards 'solving' the Quarterlife Crisis: recognition. Understanding the crisis and acknowledging its presence and its force in modern 20–35ers is fundamental, for two key reasons: it gives solidarity to the experiences of so many people who believed they were alone in their struggle to manage this phase of life; and it provides a platform from which you can then begin to tackle the crisis.

Through the course of this book, various chapters have dealt with the elements that comprise the Quarterlife Crisis, offering suggestions for managing those components. This chapter offers some general suggestions for contemplating the Quarterlife Crisis as a whole and framing its impact on your life. These are solutions, but not conclusions. They can help rationalise, mitigate and manage the Quarterlife Crisis, but they don't profess to end it – for one primary reason:

Quarterlife is a process...

... and so is the Quarterlife Crisis. There's no getting away from being 20–35, whether or not you encounter a crisis along the way. So part of dealing with a Quarterlife Crisis is a simple acceptance of its manifestation. It's not about being defeatist or pessimistic, but rather about assuming the mantle of your generation and seeing it through. Before my extensive travels, and before the full onset of my Quarterlife Crisis, I lauded structure and routine above all else. I still value those elements and attempt to insert them in my life as far as possible, but I've also learnt that there is something to be said for going with the flow.

I'll never forget the day we took a passenger boat out to a remote island in Thailand. We were dropped off on a rickety pier in the middle of a bucking sea, and walked to the only visible building on shore. No-one seemed to know of the place where we were due to be staying, although there was a great deal of hand waving and energetic gesticulating going on. After half an hour of discussions, some guy picked up our backpacks and led us back to the end of the pier, indicating that we should wait there. And wait we did. We waited until our shadows and our hair grew long. We waited until we had exhausted every memory, mind and I-spy game that we could possibly fathom. We waited until the tide rolled so far back that we could have walked to the next island, if not for the poisonous coral lining the way. Eventually a fishing boat arrived to collect us, once we had long forgotten our names and passport numbers, and took us to some vaguely distinguishable hut on the beach at the other end of the island. Lying on a particularly thin mattress that night, warm and dry if not snug and comfortable, I realised that I hadn't really had a problem spending that day in a chasm of not knowing what next; there was no choice but to pass the time. Without even being aware of it, I had simply accepted the fact that waiting it out, making the most of the day by not getting stressed about it, was the best option. Maybe I'd just spent too much time soaking up the sun and my softened brain couldn't think of another way to deal with the situation, but the experience has stuck with me nevertheless as a lesson in the value of going with the flow. And it's a strategy that can help detach some of the restless anxiety associated with the Quarterlife Crisis and its spaghetti-mix of questions.

Some parts of the crisis are simply a necessary migration through the years and phases of natural life, and, as such, are likely to stay with you as you make that journey. They are the inevitabilities: you *will* have to make some serious decisions; you *will* have to choose jobs, careers or general life pursuits; you *will* have to make changes as you get older. They are the bits that someone refers to when they shrug and say 'That's life'. The issues that are raised in the Quarterlife Crisis are seldom candidates for a 'quick fix' and often require slow and steady processing, so you'll save yourself some headaches if you reconcile yourself with that process and decide to bend with its twists and turns.

It's all relative

What also helps, although sometimes only for a fleeting moment, is to consider your plight relative to others. I was having a discussion with a particularly brilliant Quarterlifer, herself no stranger to the difficulties of this phase. She mentioned that, while she identifies with the concept of the Quarterlife Crisis and understands the uncertainty and anxiety that afflict many 20–35ers, she also sees a certain selfishness in the condition: 'If the Quarterlife Crisis is our biggest affliction, then we don't realise how lucky we are. In poor communities, young adults don't have the extravagance of too many choices regarding what to do with their lives. I remember being told that 'society buys its children the adolescence it can afford'. In poor societies children are forced to become adults even as young as in adolescence. It is only as childhood extends into what was adulthood that we have these crises about our identity. Fourteen-year-old married girls working in rice paddies have no such luxury.' At the same time, you do need to consider that all things are indeed relative; the crises the Quarterlifer faces are distressing to the individual and should not be diminished just because they aren't centred on threats to physical sustenance or saving the planet. Nevertheless, it may help the Quarterlifer who feels that the crisis is insurmountable, to take a look around and appreciate the possibility of having a choice at all.

Downtime

One of the best opportunities to take a look around and initiate some decision-making is during a period of 'downtime'. In my case, this came in the form of an unexpected operation, which had me house-ridden for a while. It was during this period that I spent most of my time in my own head, unconsciously sifting through the Quarterlife fragments that seemed to make no cohesive sense. I'm not one who can sit still for very long, and once I'd come to terms with the fact that I wasn't going back to work or doing the daily run to the grocery store just yet, I resolved to use the time productively. My downtime gave me the unbidden opportunity to contemplate my career, passion and location options, and even provided the opportunity to experiment with some practical realities. This was when I started to mould my tentative prods at the writing world into a distinct possibility. This was when I started to filter the true location options from the mass of unreal imaginings that were stressing me out. This was when I started to ask myself the hard-hitting, essential life questions that I had been eagerly trying to avoid. I didn't rush; I just initiated the process.

Certainly, taking (or being handed) some time can be most useful for reflecting and projecting. You may decide to go on a long holiday, or you may be retrenched from your job in difficult economic conditions, or you may develop a short-term case of insomnia… whatever the conditions, whether they are elected by you or inflicted on you, consider using the time to help chart the course that you would like to follow out of your Quarterlife Crisis. Identify your issues, prioritise them and their components, sift reality from unreality, and test the hypotheses of your solutions. Downtime does not necessarily have to be days, weeks or even months; it can be snatched moments or long weekends. The idea is to use the time productively to create space in your head and room to manoeuvre in and around your own Quarterlife issues.

Put pen to paper

Don't try to cross a dark minefield with a pocket flashlight. One of the best weapons of defence you have against the Quarterlife Crisis is clarity. So instead of letting your crisis issues clog up your insides, get them out into the open where you can see them and confront them. One of the best ways to do this is to write them down. Put pen to paper and list your options, questions and concerns. Writing helps extract the issues from your mind and get them out into physical space where you can see them for what they are, allowing you to be more objective about them and assess their merit. Particularly if you are the type given to excessive rumination or obsession, writing down your issues can help qualify them and stop you turning them over and over in your head where they build unnecessary momentum. Also, once you've articulated your issues and written them down, you can even quantify the options by assigning rankings or priority positions to reflect their relative importance and impact value. This may seem simplistic, but the results are certainly worthwhile: not only does it help to have your issues in written, tangible form, where you can physically juggle with them, but the actual thought processes you will need to go through to get them onto paper are valuable stepping stones on the road to resolution. The act of prioritisation will help you to form a hierarchy of sorts, so that you know where to concentrate your efforts.

You can even get started right here and now, in this book…

Attempts at permanence

The Quarterlife Crisis sits on a dais of transience: nothing feels solid or reliable. Life is changing and you are unsure of what the future holds, of what defines you, and of how to find the answers to your myriad questions. So it may help to insert a sense of permanence in your life – to put a stake in the ground from which definition can radiate. I only started to feel that I was getting a handle on my Quarterlife Crisis when I delineated the primary issues – particularly career and location – and said to myself: 'Give it a try and see how it goes.' Before that, I was working myself into a state of immobility, since each choice or option was chasing its own tail. So I eventually had to make some decisions and go with them: I chose to stay in Cape Town; I chose to give writing a chance. Whew – at least *some* decisions were tackled. And having made those choices, I had to embrace them wholeheartedly: so I had to live in Cape Town as if I was going to live here for a long time; I had to put the effort into my writing as if this was going to be my career forever. Having a clear understanding of the issues, it didn't matter so much what the realities were (i.e. that my location or my career might well change in the future); what was important was the sense of stability and permanence that began to build. From that basis, I felt that I at least had a framework within which to work. It was a start.

Especially for a 20–35er, making choices and going with them is probably more meaningful than agonising over those choices ad nauseum: you are still young enough to make a change if the choice turns out to be entirely wrong. Unless the decision is, for some reason, irreversible, then you are probably better off making a decision, going for it, and taking a realistic timeframe to evaluate it. Furthermore, I have to remember the piece of wisdom my brother always reinforces when I'm struggling with a choice between more than one option: 'if you've weighed the options, and they appear to have equal merit, then it's unlikely that one is obviously wrong; if it was, you wouldn't be toying with it in the first place – you, or someone close to you, would have noticed! You may as well choose one and go for it, because stressing about it isn't helping any longer.' So the value of inserting some permanence in your life – even if it's in the smallest measure, like buying a couch or highlighting your hair – is that it sets the ball rolling for resolution and begins to part Quarterlife's curtains of opaqueness.

Time will tell

So you step out of the hairdresser with streaks of neon blonde through your jet-black hair. Worried that you made the wrong decision? Give yourself (and your mother) time to get used to it. Sometimes decisions take a while to play themselves out and it isn't immediately evident whether they represent the right choice; you need to let them run their course while you adjust and settle into your new circumstances. Take the example of a new job. It's unlikely that you'll know on day one that this is the job for you; you'll need to take time to get to know the place, the system, the processes, the people. Give your choices a chance. Use that technique of setting ultimatums to outline an acceptable timeframe, one that will allow you to acquire a proper sense of things and endeavour to make things work before you re-evaluate your decision. Make sure that the timeframe is practical and realistic, that it balances the adequate measures of head and heart, rationale and emotion. Of course this approach has socially sensible implications, too, since it gives the impression that you aren't a quitter. It's hardly a CV builder to have left your new marketing job after a week because you didn't like your boss; maybe after a month you and your boss will have broken the ice and your job experience will have improved drastically. Indeed, only time will tell – so decide on how much time you'll allow for your decisions to take root, put a reminder in your calendar to evaluate outcomes at that date, and get on with things in the meantime.

No pain, no gain

No matter how effective your decision-making strategies, or how resourceful your anticrisis tactics, one thing is for sure: success, at whatever you are tackling, is unlikely to come without a good dose of hard work. Quarterlifers grappling with issues of 'what should I do with my life now?' sometimes entertain notions of a 'Holy Grail' as far as outcomes are concerned: simply stumbling upon the perfect job, the perfect hometown, the perfect partner. Life's reality is this: even the

'perfect' job has its down moments; even the 'perfect' home town has rainy days; even the 'perfect' partner has a habit you would prefer to change. It's less about you receiving the 'perfect' answers, and more about you making them happen. You are likely to be most successful at your career if you actively manage it. You are likely to successfully settle into your new home town if you make an effort to integrate with the community and actively enjoy the place for what it has to offer. You are likely to have a successful relationship with a partner if you actively cultivate and nurture it. Solutions – and success – will seldom fall in your lap without your own awareness and efforts. It's tempting to look at someone else's life and say 'things just work out for them', but in all likelihood, that person has put a whole lot of effort into *making* things work out for him/her. Rather than letting the Quarterlife Crisis wash over you in great waves and dump you on the shore, realise that it is your action and reaction that will help you overcome it; that the 'perfect' outcomes are of your own making; and that 'close to perfect' is good, too.

Positive reinforcement

Since the Quarterlife Crisis can be overwhelming, it is often difficult to remain objective about your situation. Yet that approach of playing an observer's role is precisely the type of perspective a Quarterlifer needs to gain in order to expedite solutions to the crisis. On top of that is the need for positive reinforcement whereby you congratulate yourself on the parts of your life that you feel are going well and encourage yourself to actively manage the parts that may need some help. The fundamentals of psychology include that very concept of positive reinforcement: actions or attitudes which promote desired behaviours through positive response. Pavlov did so for his dogs; primary caregivers do so for their children; you must do so for your Quarterlifer self. So you decide to take up a career in photojournalism: talk about it, join a chat room, buy the t-shirt, promote yourself to yourself.

The trials of Quarterlife can deplete your confidence resources, so you may need to forcefully rebuild them. Try to look at your own situation and choices independently, and reward that which is reward-worthy. In fact, applying a technique that writer Anne Schuster has developed in her writing courses to gain perspective on a personal situation, is quite useful here, too: write / talk / think about a circumstance as if you are living it in the moment. Then stand back and provide some background for that circumstance, using an insider's access to information to provide contextual detail. Then stand back even further and evaluate the circumstance as an outsider. This layering effect will help you distance yourself from the emotions of Quarterlife that can cloud your judgement or overwhelm you, and will help outline the positive elements of your situation that should sustain and support you.

Redefining the Quarterlife 'Crisis'

We may have made things harder for ourselves by calling this Quarterlife situation a 'crisis', since the word has such harsh connotations. Of all the synonyms for 'crisis' – disaster, catastrophe, emergency, calamity – I think that the ones that come closest to the Quarterlifer's situation are words like 'predicament' or 'dilemma' since they detract from the severity of a 'crisis'. While I'm not saying that we should change the term or diminish the extent of discomfort, anxiety, doubt and fear that are certainly indicative of many Quarterlifer's situations, I wonder whether, in the bid for solutions, we shouldn't try to redefine 'crisis' and, in so doing, take the emphasis off the diseased, calamitous undertones. This isn't about saying that 'there is no such thing as crisis for a Quarterlifer' – if I believed that, I wouldn't have written this book – but rather about saying that having recognised such a condition, let's lessen its negativity by reframing the words we use to describe it. This is a bit like switching on the lights when you thought there was a monster in the room, or reminding yourself that the ghosts in the Haunted House ride at the carnival are really people in dress-up and masks. What we're aiming to do is to deconstruct the Quarterlife Crisis so that it becomes tolerable, manageable and overcomeable!

So instead of thinking of the Quarterlife Crisis as a Quarterlife Catastrophe or a Quarterlife Tragedy, try think of it as a Quarterlife Dilemma or a Quarterlife Quandary, particularly since you are unlikely to get through the Quarterlife phase without hitting some predicaments along the way – that's just the nature of being 20–35, and you aren't alone. By shifting your perspective on the 'crisis', you may start to shift your approach for dealing with it towards a more proactive, positive stance. And when the going gets really tough, and you feel closer to disaster than dilemma... then re-read this book!

My tub of frozen yoghurt is melting faster than the sidewalks on a steamy New York City summer's day; but I like it better that way – slightly soft, almost drink-able, but still with enough body left to slide its slow vanilla roll down the back of my throat. I've had a love affair with this frozen treat since the first sample I tasted while I was at university: my friends bought me litres of it for my 21st, 22nd and 23rd birthday presents and I savoured every last drop. I carried my obsession with 'froz yog' (as I affectionately termed it) right on into my late-twenties and consider myself somewhat of a connoisseur on the stuff. It has been a constant companion: through celebratory and miserable moments, through graduation, interviews, jobs, travels (although it was a bit hard to come by in Mongolia, but I carried my 'frozen yoghurt frequent buyer's' card with me all the same), and marriage. I know I will always love it, and unless some sadistic monster takes it off the market forever, a few quiet moments with a froz-yog tub will always be my tonic. So I'm sitting with a particu-larly large bucket of it today, on my birthday, as I head closer to the exit door from the twenties, leaving age 21 as a bright shining pebble slowly gathering dust.

I swallow a spoonful and look out the window towards the sea. It's a gorgeous spring day in Cape Town, approximating summer but without the hordes of tourists and hiked-up prices. I've spent the last two hours tidying the apartment, feeling a little warm glow when I remember what someone said to me a few nights ago: she had never been to the apartment before and she smiled when she walked in and looked around: 'This is a real home,' she commented. I like that – that we've managed to make a 'real home' in the relatively short amount of time since we returned from our travels and decided to settle in South Africa. 'She's right', I think to myself, 'The place does feel comfortingly familiar, warmly welcoming. It does feel like home.' Another spoonful, this time of the chocolate flavour, and I nudge the framed wedding photos on the bookcase back into position. I still sometimes can't believe that I'm married, but the idea has definitely started to take root and I've stopped staring at my wedding ring with googly-eyed disbelief. I'm adjusting, steadily, to the changes that marriage has brought about in my life and am enjoying leaning on its granite sense of permanence.

A ringing phone disturbs my reverie: 'Hi Jo, happy birthday!' It's my old manager, a colleague from my past life in management consulting. We've kept in contact and often chat about her work, my work, work in general. Today is no different, except at the end of the conversation she asks: 'So when are you are coming back to consulting? Haven't you had enough of this writing thing?' And I realise, with that same element of self-surprise that keeps alerting me to my Quarterlife issues and outcomes, that I haven't had enough of this writing thing. 'I've got a way to go still before I abandon this ship,' I tell her. 'I said I'd give myself six months or so, to see how it went, and I'm still happy. So I'll keep pushing it.' Interesting things happen when you mix passion with career. I can hardly believe how much I've enjoyed the whole career shift. And if that gratification changes at any time, I'll just have to deal with it, creating and using the necessary resources.

Tub of frozen yoghurt finished, I go to the bathroom to wipe my sticky face – I do tend to let my enthusiasm for the substance get the better of me! I catch myself in the mirror and groan – another zit. It seems that I'm still not too old for pimples! Well, maybe I should start embracing them as evidence of being young at heart rather than bemoaning my wretched fate every time they erupt, volcanically, on the surface of my skin. I'm physically restraining myself from performing DIY plastic surgery when the phone rings again; this time, it's a friend living in Australia. 'So when are you coming to join us here, Jo? Any time soon?'

Somehow, I think that the questions about my career, my location, my procreation plans and my thoughts about the future will never really abate, at least not for the next few years as parameters continue to change and decisions continue to be made. I just have to stop letting those questions bother me, and focus on the answers that I've already come up with and the burning issues I am in the process of resolving. People seem to accept an answer if you say it with enough conviction. Since I've resolved to live in South Africa, people are happier to accept the decision if I throw my full support behind it. Moreover, saying it with assurance has also helped me to commit to the decision and make it work. 'You know,' I tell my friend, 'I'm happy where I am right now. So this is where I'm staying.'

I don't, for a second, think that everything is decided, organised, settled and resolved. I don't think that the elements of my Quarterlife Crisis that so consumed me are now all done and dusted. I'm sure that pieces of them will arise again, at points in the future, when there are decisions to be made or changes to be managed. For some of the issues that I've unearthed, I chose procrastination

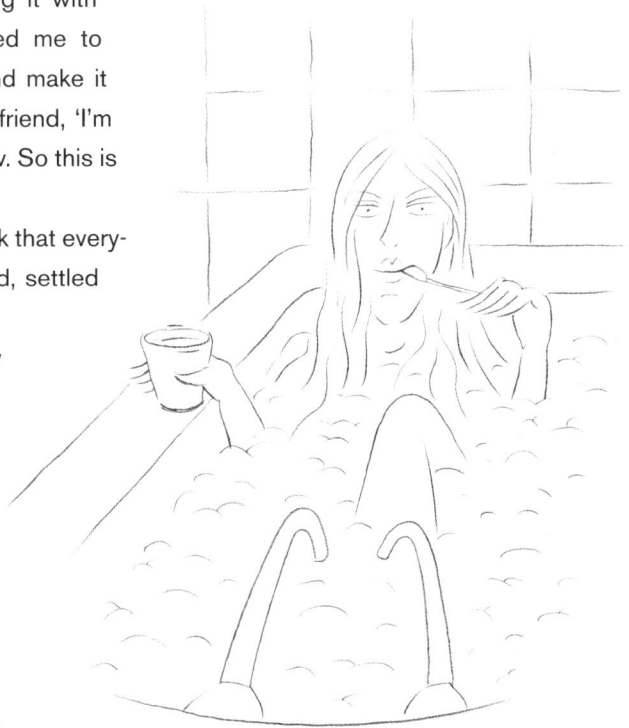

over resolution, so I know that I will need to tackle those issues more firmly when they become pressing again. And I will: I'll arm myself with a tub of frozen yoghurt, make sure the geyser is full for plenty of hot bubble baths, and face whatever relics emerge from my Quarterlife Crisis. Not all the doors are closed. But I was the one who chose not to close them: despite the fact that options are what can make Quarterlife difficult, I still left some options open because, in manageable measures, they also represent flexibility and freedom. Now is not the time in my life to be closing all doors and battening down the hatches; I am still young, able to adapt, with few strings attached. As those characteristics change, so too will my decisions and attitudes to reflect the relevant consequences. I have had to identify the elements of my Quarterlife Crisis that were causing me the most discomfort, and seek to resolve them so that I could alleviate the feelings of rootlessness, indecision and self-doubt that overwhelmed me. Now that I've fitted some of the pieces of the Quarterlife puzzle together, I can lie low and enjoy them. Because change, like death and taxes, is certain. Things change; people change. That's life. That's Quarterlife.

Ever since I became aware of my own Quarterlife Crisis, acknowledging the issues that were troubling me, I've been focused on how to get around them. Writing this book was part of that process, since through it I came into contact with scores of other Quarterlifers' stories and was forced to hold a magnifying glass over my own issues. In fact, while I was researching and writing this manuscript, I planned to use the title 'Surviving Quaterlife' for the book. But working through it – both the book and my Quarterlife Crisis – I've come to realise that 'survival' is something that victims do: you 'survive' a plane crash, or a life-threatening illness, or a situation beyond your control. But Quarterlife is none of those things, primarily since you can ultimately exercise your own control over it. Yes, it overwhelms and engulfs you to the point that it may feel unmanageable, but there certainly are positive techniques, attitudes and mindsets that you can adopt to overcome it. 'Surviving Quarterlife' is about getting *inside* Quarterlife: about getting to know it, and yourself, thoroughly and completely; about understanding the issues that plague you – their source, their roots in social expectations, their impact; about facing your demons and your pimples; about finding your hot baths and frozen yoghurt, the comfort factors and resources of strength that fortify you; and about taking proactive steps to manage your crisis. It's not about rolling over and playing the 'poor me' game, letting time and tide wash over you. Coming to terms with the Quarterlife Crisis is an active process of acceptance, understanding and resolution.

While I certainly cannot offer exhaustive or finite solutions to the dilemmas that Quarterlifers face, I can share my own experience of the crisis together with the answers that I have found to be useful, and hope that others find the observations and resolutions equally constructive. While I believe that each Quarterlife Crisis is unique to the individual, I also believe that there are some fundamental truths that every Quarterlifer can add to their arsenal of crisis- (and life-) management mechanisms. From a personal point of view, the 'survival' is in understanding the crisis, mitigating the anxiety associated with it, taking some firm steps to clear a path, and surrounding myself with people who support me as I go with the flow. The Quarterlife Crisis is a process: it tends to have an unnoticed beginning, an uncomfortable middle and a manageable end. The crisis needs to run its course and you need to take comfort in knowing that its manifestation in your life is not an aberration or a stigma – it is a norm.

Ultimately, overcoming the Quarterlife Crisis is both an achievement and a necessity: the former, because it takes some really hard work to make your way through the process of Quarterlife, and the latter because you actually have no choice but to do so if you want to successfully navigate the course of your life. Most importantly, is the resounding 'must' that applies to the Quarterlife Crisis: it must be lived, explored, tolerated. It will not be resolved through disregard, it will not be mitigated through intolerance, and there are few fast tracks through the experience. The Quarterlife Crisis is a modern rite of passage. It is not a disease to be cured, or a plague to be eradicated. It is a condition of experience and, for many, an inevitable prerequisite for the future.

Acknowledgements

I don't know about you, but I always look through the 'Acknowledgements' section of books that I read. And I always leave that section till last. I regard the 'Acknowledgements' as something of an insider's view: both of the making of the book, and of the author's own personal existence. That's why I wait until I've completed my reading – by then, I feel that I have at least some understanding of the person who penned the words and therefore hold more of an interest in the people and processes that helped the writer along the way. Also, the 'Acknowledgements' section is such a public place. The sentiments that the author expresses there hold immense significance for those who are acknowledged because the appreciation and recognition are laid bare for the entire world to see. Seldom do we get the chance to publicly acknowledge the people who make a difference in the great rough and tumble of our lives, so I'd like to grab this chance with all ten typing fingers.

Without my husband, Richard, this book would never have seen the light of day. Thank you for insisting that I give 'this writing thing' a chance, for your unwavering support through the process, for your regular chapter reviews (I noticed that you always followed any negative criticism with a positive one to make sure that I never lost heart!), and for always helping me push the boundaries.

To Roofrack and Izabella, who made sure that I got fresh air and lots of laughs for inspiration: I now know the easiest way to come through the chaos of Quarterlife… get a dog!

For a constant source of encouragement and take-your-mind-off-it humour, I have always turned to my father, Cecil. But his support in the conception and birth of this book superseded all expectations. Papa, your input into this process has been invaluable: your ideas, business advice, and endlessly quotable observations have been indispensable. And now that it's all done, you actually do have to read the entire book – yourself!

Equally vital has been my mother's involvement in this process. From extensive editing and proof-reading, to always hearing out my ideas and fears, you, yourself, are an inspiration. You gave me the wherewithal to tackle this project, as all others, and helped me keep a cool head through my own Quarterlife Crisis. Thank you.

To my Granny Annie, who was always fascinated that I had the gall to write this book, I say this: I got my guts from you! They might not have had Quarterlife Crises back home in Russia, but that never stopped you from patting mine on the back and sending it straight to bed with chicken soup and chocolates every time it reared its head!

To Dr Aneta Shaw, who reviewed this book from a psychological point of view and verified that I was, indeed, within my right mind: thank you for your unselfish time and your crucial input.

To Linda de Villiers, Ethné Clarke, Lesley Joubert, Sean Robertson, David du Plessis and all New Holland Publishing associates who believe in this project and have guided me through an unfamiliar world: here's a huge 'thank you' and an even huger 'hoorah!'

To Marcus Brewster and my personal PR team of siblings, family and friends who started publicising this book before I had even finished writing it: thanks for the resounding vote of confidence! I hope it meets your expectations. In particular, thanks to Jonny Abitz for your regular flow of articles, statistics and ideas, and for your constant interest in the process. Thanks also to Lisa Thomas for your critical review at the early stages and your willing ear throughout the journey!

To my Quarterlifer peers, and to those whose stories and experiences adorn these pages: my deepest gratitude for the inspiration, the sharing and the solidarity. For those who kept asking when this book was coming out: Well, here it is! I hope it helps!

Finally, to my fear of failure, my 'impostor complex', my cluttered study, and, grandest of all, my Quarterlife Crisis: thanks for the ride, but it's time for me to be on my way.